KEND

HEALING
STEPS

EMBRACING GOD'S CARING
PRESENCE WHILE WALKING
THROUGH BETRAYAL TRAUMA

Trilogy Christian Publishers
A Wholly Owned Subsidiary of Trinity Broadcasting Network
2442 Michelle Drive
Tustin, CA 92780
Copyright © 2024 by Kendra Lee
Scripture quotations marked NLT are taken from the Holy Bible, New Living Translation, copyright © 1996, 2004, 2015 by Tyndale House Foundation. Used by permission of Tyndale House Publishers, Inc., Carol Stream, Illinois 60188. All rights reserved.
All rights reserved, including the right to reproduce this book or portions thereof in any form whatsoever.
For information, address Trilogy Christian Publishing
Rights Department, 2442 Michelle Drive, Tustin, CA 92780.
Trilogy Christian Publishing/ TBN and colophon are trademarks of Trinity Broadcasting Network.
For information about special discounts for bulk purchases, please contact Trilogy Christian Publishing.

Trilogy Disclaimer: The views and content expressed in this book are those of the author and may not necessarily reflect the views and doctrine of Trilogy Christian Publishing or the Trinity Broadcasting Network.

10 9 8 7 6 5 4 3 2 1
Library of Congress Cataloging-in-Publication Data is available.

B-ISBN#: 979-8-89333-009-0
E-ISBN#: 979-8-89333-010-6

DEDICATION

I want to dedicate this book to my Paraclete, the Holy Spirit, who I got to know during my Ironman training. You biked, swam, and ran with me—the hours we spent talking. You have been there through each terrible day of discovering I've been betrayed. In the recovery community, these days are known as "destruction days." Even when I pushed you away, you wouldn't leave. You have been my rock. You taught me to stand firm, helped me to memorize Romans 8, and gave me strength to get back up. You have taught me to remain teachable and humble. You have told me when to speak and when to shut up. You laugh with me and at me. We are so connected at the hip. I am forever grateful. You are a true friend. I love you.

FOREWORD

The bulk of my professional career has been spent working with people who were trying to reconcile and restore marriages that appeared to be irreparably damaged. This eyewitness account describes such a marriage.

One of the lessons I have learned is that if such a marriage is to be reconciled, it is through the Hand of God working in the marriage. As you read the pages of this book, look for the God sightings.

If you picked up this book because your marriage is troubled, pay special attention to the instruments God used to work in this marriage. Consider the obstacles that had to be overcome. Do any of them sound familiar? Consider outside assistance (professional and otherwise). Could you engage such aid? Consider the attributes that were instrumental in reconciling the marriage. Do you need to reconsider your mindset, desires, intents, or actions?

The printed words reflect how the author speaks (and lives), full of energy and vitality. It makes for a very interesting and moving read.

The pages that follow are a story and testimony to be enjoyed by anyone who reads them. They will also be an encouragement to all who read. The pages are also intended to serve as a blueprint for anyone who would like to build up a marriage.

Timothy B. Visser

PREFACE

This book came into being when God showed up and impressed upon me that I'd be OK. Not many women are willing to share their journey. I have found a few of "us" betrayed partners want to stay hidden in embarrassment and shame. We have horrible thoughts and questions enter our minds, and we wonder things like, "How did this happen?" or, "Am I stupid for believing my spouse?" and, "Did I pick a bad husband?" or "What will people think?"

Yes, there are a lot of books to help us betrayed partners. But not many share their ugly journey of survival. I want to encourage women. I want betrayed spouses to know they are normal. I have been there and have been hurt, angry, sad, confused, shocked, and insane. I want betrayed spouses to know God sees them. He will meet you wherever you are. He truly cares. My story is a God story of how He showed up for me. I want to let you know He still does miracles. He still changes people. I am miracle #one. My husband is miracle #two. God is the hero of my story and yours, too!

ACKNOWLEDGMENTS

First, I'd like to thank my editor and TBN/Trilogy for allowing me to share my story.

My four therapists are Susan, Alaina, Tina, and Michelle. I am so grateful to all of you for helping me on my journey forward and getting the healing I needed. I appreciate your wisdom!

To the group I never wanted to be in, my wives of addicts group- I love you all. Your realness, your vulnerability. I have felt loved by each of you. Thanks for supporting me, encouraging me, and validating me.

My lawyer, Tim, who showed me how to pray BIG prayers and who sent me verses like Micah 7:7 (NLT), "But as for me, I watch in hope for the Lord, I wait for God my Savior; my God will hear me." Thank you for all your wisdom as I walked the divorce road. For meeting me in my pain. For your patience, prayers, and encouragement. Thank you for writing the forward of this book and for believing in me.

My walking friend, Carol, who became a prayer warrior for me. I love our God story of how we met. God knew I needed you. Thank you for all the hours you spent listening and encouraging me as we walked together. Thank you for walking my dog when I just couldn't.

To my gym friends, Dan, Lucy, and Joan, whom I felt safe to share with. Thanks for being in my classes and becoming my prayer partners.

To the rest of my fifty prayer partners who rallied around me, never left my side, prayed like crazy, read my updates, checked in, supported, and encouraged me and my husband. You are my safe people!

I am thankful for Room 2 Heal for hosting my addict husband. For Coach Andrew, for being there for my husband, and for Coach Lisa, for guiding me in the support I needed as a betrayed wife.

To my bestie, Karen, who has been my support and friend since 1998. For all your prayers, encouragement, and many handwritten cards you have sent. Thank you for all the meals you prepped for me, the flowers you gave, the precious hugs, and many hours of listening and crying with me!

To my other bestie, Melissa, who always answers her phone when I call, who always gives me a new perspective, helps keep me grounded, is always up for an early dinner, and has taught me much about laughter.

To Dodie, my 4 am prayer partner. We have talked daily for years through numerous difficult roads. I love how God has weaved us together to pray for each other. I look forward to my daily text. "This is our story."

To Lindsay, my daily check-in prayer partner. What a privilege to walk with you on your own road of suffering with your child. I am grateful we can pray for each other daily.

To Amanda, my prayer warrior. My support no matter what choice I make. You go before God and ask Him. Thank you for not leaving my side but for drawing even closer. I am blessed.

To Lily, who has taken much of her time in college to teach me about grammar. Thanks for being brave and reading this book. For your hours spent editing. Thanks for always making me laugh. "Me and you, a two-man crew. Side by side, we're unified, and we will never be divided. Win or lose, we go in twos. We're the best of buddies. Me and you." Thanks for all your hugs.

To my precious sister, Shelby, who became my best friend during this journey. Thanks for coming near and holding me dear. You cried with me, prayed with me, and empathized with me. I appreciate all your vulnerability. I love the bond we share. Never forget "Fred," our cardinal friend. I'm excited to see where your healing journey takes you!

My favorite aunt, Vicki. I love being related to you! I love how much we are alike with our music (70s), clothes, laughter, salt, butter, books, and love for God. You have become my protector, prayer warrior, and biggest cheerleader ever! I love your zest for life and have learned much about grace from you! Thanks for always giving me the right scripture verse when needed! I want to be like you when I grow up, but please understand that I just can't seem to get into Rod Stewart. Sorry.

My precious five children and their spouses, Justin (Christina), Brittany, Cassie, Bailee (Dylan), and Lily, thank you for covering your mom in prayer as you watched over 20 years of this destruction. Thank you for learning about God right alongside me. For the many, many hugs and tears. For your beautiful smiles. Each one of you is a picture of grace. Stay close to each other; remember you are all best friends! Stay faithful to our Holy God.

My eight grandbabies who bring such joy and give me a reason to smile daily! May you never get tired of hearing Mami's story and God's faithfulness.

Thank you to my parents for your love and support and for teaching me about prayer. For always praying for me!

To my wonderful husband and partner on this roller coaster ride. I am grateful for your bravery to get the much-needed help. I am grateful for your surrender to this process of recovery and for your testimony of what God can do through recovery. For your bravery of jumping into the unknown. I am grateful to witness your heart transformation and your sanity being restored! Thank you for giving me the gift of staying home with our beautiful children and homeschooling. Thanks for staying curious with me! Thanks for supporting my recovery and healing journey. Thanks for your full support of this book!

To my Lord and Savior, Jesus Christ, who has shown me much grace and forgiveness, Who has wrapped me in His loving arms, Who has pulled me close, Who has endured much screaming and crying and didn't run away. Thank you for all the cuddles at night and talks during the day. Thanks for leading me on this journey and for flooding my brain with ideas. Thank you for your patience. Thank you for my salvation. I can't wait to sit at your feet soon and get a real hug!

INTRODUCTION

I wish in this book I could give you a step-by-step formula for walking through betrayal trauma and how to overcome Complex PTSD, etc. But there is no formula. I can, however, allow my story to encourage you. I can tell you that God is with you, sees, loves, and won't ever leave you. I will promise you that you will be changed on this road. There is no stopping that. This road will be a blessing to you– if you stay curious.

We all suffer in this life, some more than others. I have been on this journey for over 20 years until I got the help I desperately needed. I have not "arrived" but have survived. I am here to tell you that you are a survivor, also.

I want to encourage you that God is on this horrible road with you. You may not feel Him sometimes, but He is there holding your hand.

As you read my journey, ask God to show you new things about Him.

You are brave, strong, and courageous.

TABLE OF CONTENTS

1 - God is My Surgeon 23

2 - God of Hagar 31

3 - God of My Prayers 35

4 - God of My Battlefield 45

5 - God of My Broken Heart. 49

6 - God of My Father Abraham. 55

7 - God is my Handyman 59

8 - God is My Safety. 63

9 - God is My Shepherd 67

10 - God of My Chaos 73

11 - God is My Detangler 77

12 - God of My Grief 87

13 - The God of My Losses 103

14 - God of My Emotions. 109

15 - God of My Emotions Part 2. 121

16 - God is My Comfort 125

17 - God of My Dares 129

18 - God of My Garden 135

19 - God of My Body 141

20 - God of my Sanity (and Insanity) 147

21 - God of My Laughter 155

22 - God of my Intimacy 159

23 - God is My Friend 165

24 - God of My Whys 171

25 - God of My Triggers 177

26 - God is my Living Water 183

27 - God of My Gratitude 187

28 - God of My Redemption Story 191

29 - God of My Miracles 199

30 - God of my Forgiveness 205

PROLOGUE

At age 16, I discovered I was pregnant. I was put under church discipline and then kicked out of my Christian school. A few months later, I entered the marriage covenant full of shame in a cream dress, not white, to show I was not a virgin. I hate that dress. I felt condemned for years after getting married because of what I had done. Nonetheless, I had always wanted to be a wife and mom. So, I was happy to be married and expecting! We moved 90 minutes from my hometown, found an apartment, a church, and a small group, and started our life together, thinking it would be "Happily Ever After." He worked two jobs, and went to school, and I worked part-time.

As we added two more children and became a family of five, we moved to a new state in 1998. Fast forward to 2001, My husband had a great job. I stayed home with our children and homeschooled. I was living my dream! We just had our 4th child when the first catastrophic event destroyed our marriage. More catastrophic events would hit me throughout 2001-2021 and served to reveal the shame of the cream dress that I'd never dealt with. This is my journey of clinging to God and what that means. I call this my "Red Sea Journey." A journey of faith, letting go, learning, survival, and flourishing.

1

GOD IS MY SURGEON

I had no choice in the matter... a bomb was hiding in my house. My husband planted it and hid it. He thought he could keep it safe until one day, in the summer of 2001, he confessed to me his affairs and secret lifestyle. I sat there stunned, unable to move or breathe. He wanted out of the lifestyle, but we had no clear direction on getting him the help he needed. Little did I know throughout the next 20 years, there would be more bombs.

One day, I decided to draw a picture of how it felt to be betrayed. I pictured my husband handing me a bomb, and it exploded in my face. I felt I was ruined. How could someone I love do this to me? It's genuinely how I felt about his sex addiction and all the lies. *Boom.* In one poof, everything was gone—house, family, memories... even me. I was left powerless. I hate powerlessness.

As a child, I was powerless when I was sexually abused. As an adult, I sought that power and control by finding safety in my disciplined life. *Boom.* The person who was supposed to make me feel safe did the *un*thinkable. *Boom–* I died. I changed that day. Many betrayed spouses call this *destruction day*, or D-day for short.

I imagined turning into a caterpillar that went right into a cocoon. I was NOT coming out. I scrambled to keep normal... whatever normal was. I wanted my kids and my family. I needed friends and self-care. As I was trying to make sense of everything I felt, I realized I needed a community of other wives who were hurting like me.

I tried to avoid any change for my body's sake. On the outside, I was "fine." But I had no inside. I was empty and broken. I cried alone– a lot. Has anyone seen me? I felt lost. I was scared. My foundation was ripped from under me without permission. My reality was gone. My identity was gone. I needed oxygen– *now*.

Little did I know that God would meet me in my cocoon. God knew where I was. He crawled into the cocoon with me that day. God reminded me that I was still His. I wasn't lost. He sees me. He is El Roi– The God who sees. He brought His healing balm to me. The balm of Gilead (Jeremiah 8:22). *He* was Jehovah Rappha– My healer. God loves messes, and this one was a doozy.

GOD IS MY SURGEON

That day, God reminded me who I was.

As a child of God, you are:

1. Loved: You are deeply loved by God, who considers you His precious child and desires a close relationship with you.

2. Accepted: You are accepted and embraced by God– just as you are with all your strengths and weaknesses.

3. Forgiven: Through the sacrifice of Jesus Christ, you are offered forgiveness for your sins. You have the opportunity to experience spiritual renewal and reconciliation with God.

4. Chosen: You are chosen by God to be part of His family. To participate in His kingdom and to carry out His purposes on earth.

5. Empowered: You have the Holy Spirit dwelling within you, empowering you to live a life that honors God, to grow in faith, and to make a positive impact in the world.

6. Secure: You are assured of God's faithfulness and promise never to leave nor forsake you. You can find comfort and security knowing you are held in God's loving hands.

7. Called: You have a unique calling and purpose in God's plan. He has equipped you with gifts, talents, and opportunities to contribute to His kingdom and to bring about positive change in

the lives of others.

Thank you for making me so wonderfully complex! Your workmanship is marvelous- how well I know it. You watched me as I was being formed in utter seclusion, as I was woven together in the dark of the womb. You saw me before I was born. Every day of my life was recorded in your book. Every moment was laid out before a single day had passed. How precious are your thoughts about me, O God. They cannot be numbered!

Psalms 139:14-18 (NLT)

From the beginning, I have been formed by God. I am created in *His* image. I am here to bring Him glory. This life was not about me. My suffering was not about me. The God who made the world was walking closely with me, step by step. The oxygen He gave me was called GRACE. Boy, did I breathe it in… soaked in it, rolled around in it, and drank it. I consumed so much grace I felt guilty! I wasn't dying. I was becoming. The surgeon was now performing surgery on my heart. It was going to take a while. Am I willing?

I was going to come out beautiful again with a new heart! The word *acceptance* helped me change my perspective— accepting what I cannot change even though I didn't want to. Accepting that the old me was gone– the old marriage gone, old husband gone, old family gone. Everything, and I mean *everything,* was different. Could this surgeon resurrect me

GOD IS MY SURGEON

again? Would I come out OK? Was I willing to go through the painful surgery of transforming? Would I even like my new self? Would my family, friends, kids like me? Could I trust anyone? I clung to Christ and wrapped myself in his robe of righteousness. Acceptance is challenging, yet bitterness/denial is even more challenging. My identity in Christ never changed. But who I was changed. I am scared of change. Nonetheless, God crawled into my cocoon with me. I was transformed in that cocoon. He was in the process of reviving me. He said change is good.

Let's look at scripture:

- Psalms 31:9- David is in such distress from grief. Let's assume he felt lost and confused.

- 1 Kings 19- Elijah flees to the wilderness (into a cocoon). He is scared and lonely– lost.

- Job also expressed loss over losing his health, wealth, and family. My heart aches for this man and his wife.

Did Jesus feel lost? He was in such deep distress as he was in the garden. He understands. He was choosing to lose himself for me so I may have eternity. Also, I believe such a loss fell upon Jesus when God forsook him, a true abandonment. This revealing of what happened between God and his Son makes me quiver. I can't even think about it without crying—the most significant loss, even if not for long. What I do know is that Jesus does understand abandonment. Jesus understands feeling lost. I am so grateful I will never know abandonment from God because of Jesus.

Jesus came to give us a new life, a new identity. Jesus specializes in helping us change! There are stories in the bible where God has performed surgery and brought about heart change. (I will talk about Judah later.) He is my surgeon, and I will never be the same.

Do you feel lost? Are you ready to start this new chapter of your life? Draw a picture of something that you can write ten things about who you are in Christ. (rainbow, caterpillar, butterfly, flowers, sun). Meditate on it and give praise. Let's look up John 15:15, 1 Peter 2:9, and Galatians 4:7. What do they say about who you are? Nothing can change our identity in Him. We are secure.

When you have time. Or when you want to. Write a goodbye letter to yourself. Next, write a letter to yourself to read a year from now on who you hope to become.

He is your Jehovah Rappha.

You are healed.

Jeremiah 30:17

GOD IS MY SURGEON

2

GOD OF HAGAR

I have always loved Hagar in the Bible. No one talks about her. She was a slave girl from Egypt given to Sarah between the ages of 14-20. Due to Sarah's inability to have children, Sarah gives Hagar to Abraham as a wife. She was used for Sarah's plan.

Hagar becomes pregnant and poses a threat to Sarah. Can you see the jealousy that was stirred? Sarah most likely began comparing herself to Hagar-- a young, beautiful, and pregnant woman. Comparing myself with women and seeing them as threats resonates with me.

Hagar ended up having the firstborn son of Abraham. Do you wonder if Sarah felt useless now? I can't imagine how hard this was for both Sarah and Hagar. But Hagar must have been a praying woman, for it says, "God answered her prayer."

What emotions do you think Hagar felt? Put yourself in her shoes. She must have felt grieved, angry, sad, lonely, rejected, abandoned, betrayed, unworthy, unloved, unseen, regretful, and violated...to name a few.

What emotions come up for you right now in this season of life? Can you tell God?

Hagar didn't ask for any of this, yet God met her. She is the only person who gave God a name! She calls Him *El Roi* (The God who sees). Then, God tells her that He would bless her descendants (the same blessing He gave Abraham). She would be a mother of nations! She left the dessert that day a bold, courageous woman. She now has renewed hope! This is what an encounter with God can do.

God saw and heard her. He met her by the spring. Even though she was in despair and rejected, He comforted her. Guess what? God sees *us*! He wants our fears and tears. God showed compassion to an outsider– a slave and a woman. He also desires to show compassion to us.

Hagar receives instructions from God to return to Abraham's house to fulfill the blessing and He also assures her of protection. She obeys.

Hagar shows us that God draws near to us even when we wander in wilderness places– even when life circumstances and systems of power push us down and toss us out. Do you feel God is drawing you near?

What names of God comfort you in this season right now? How has God met you in your disaster? Do you believe He sees you just like He saw Hagar? Let these truths bring you comfort.

Consider getting something for yourself to remember this precious journey between you and God. It doesn't have to be significant. I bought myself a ring with three pink stones to represent the Trinity and how He's walked beside me on this journey.

When you have time, draw a picture of yourself sitting in your destruction– draw a picture of eyes looking at you from the sky! Because a holy God sees you. What are some ways you can praise Him today?

Because of Christ, we hope for eternal glory. He will meet you. How does this truth help you endure this suffering?

You are seen.

Genesis 16:13

3

GOD OF MY PRAYERS

Did you know God loves fragrance? He created our sense of smell. Many verses talk about our sacrifices being a fragrance to God.

Leviticus 3:5– "And Aaron's sons will burn them on top of the burnt offering on the wood burning on the altar. It is a special gift, a pleasing aroma to the Lord." (NLT)

2 Corinthians 2:15– "Our lives are a Christ-like fragrance rising up to God. But this fragrance is perceived differently by those who are being saved and by those who are perishing." (NLT)

Ephesians 5:2– "Live a life filled with love, following the example of Christ. He loved us and offered himself as a sacrifice for us, a pleasing aroma to God." (NLT)

HEALING STEPS

Were you aware that your prayers have a sweet aroma?

Revelation 5:8– "And when he took the scroll, the four living beings and the twenty-four elders fell down before the Lamb. Each one had a harp, and they held gold bowls filled with incense, which are the prayers of God's people." (NLT).

When I was first married, I met a sweet wife who would hold me accountable to pray for my husband daily. Thirty-five years later, I still do. I then moved away and found another precious, homeschooling mom who decided we should fast one day a week for our kids for their purity, salvation, and protection. I'm still doing that, too. I didn't even know it was a sweet aroma to God. All I knew was that I needed God's grace in my family as I raised five kids and had a crazy marriage.

From the beginning, prayer/fasting helped build my foundation on the rock (God). God was helping me build my faith muscle. Prayer is a mindset that works against the enemy. Satan loves to target the mind– especially a weak mind. My prayers started as, "Please help this and that." and turned into crying and begging prayers. My list of prayers and people to pray for became overwhelming. Prayer started to exhaust me, yet I also looked forward to my time with God and having intentional time with my Father.

I learned the most about prayer after my two miscarriages.

GOD OF MY PRAYERS

I learned how to cling to God during the process of losing my first baby. I kept praying and asking God not to allow that again. However, it wasn't until the next miscarriage that got my attention, and I started to question God during my prayers. I thought, *I am a faithful warrior who doesn't deserve this. Come on, God!*

By the time I was pregnant again after my second miscarriage, I felt surrendered entirely. I didn't have much faith, just more fear. I was just expecting a 3rd miscarriage. But God understood my small faith. He allowed me to carry #4 and #5 to full term. But, little did I know the first tornado was about to hit.

When child #4 was one year old, I had my first D-day. My husband said he had something to tell me. I ran all four kids over to the neighbors. I sat there while he shared with me how he had been visiting clubs and parlors. *Wait,* I thought, *I'm a praying wife!* I screamed at God. I have been praying for protection for my husband and our marriage for years. I was fasting! Was God not listening? I was left in confusion about prayer. But I continued to stay faithful. I wore my armor and kept asking, begging, and crying for God. My prayers became more daring. I drew closer to God as He continued to show me about Him. Prayer was a habit. I wasn't going to quit. God was slowly showing me that He wasn't my "genie". My prayers consisted of asking, surrendering, and praising.

But it wasn't until the 3rd D-day (2015) when I saw on

HEALING STEPS

the phone bill that he had been chatting a lot with someone. So I called her. That is when I went into a downward spiral. "Not again Lord."

I ended up depressed and wanted to walk away from God. I didn't care who God was. I was dying. My foundation felt like it was crumbling, and I wanted to quit fighting for my marriage. Even though I told God I was done, God used that 3rd "tornado" and my depression to make my foundation even more substantial. How dare He?

In 2018, I was in training for a full Ironman. Triathletes cannot have headphones on any triathlon course. So, I used that time to pray and encourage people on the course. This full Ironman was *long*. I fell in love with my paraclete, the Holy Spirit, who trained with me daily. Swimming, biking, and running. Me and Him. We had the best time. I'd talk to Him, ask Him questions, share my life, and pray for many others on the course. I also memorized Romans 8 to recite to help the time go by. This training helped me with my mindset work.

I was out on the course for 15 hours that day, and He was with me the entire time. He gave me strength and energy the entire day. Twice, my family didn't think I was going to finish because I was running out of time. But my paraclete took care of me. Reminding me to change gears or run faster. I learned then to truly be okay with quiet and be alone with my mind, to pray about everything out there on the course! Little did I know that this prayer time with the

Holy Spirit was about building my foundation stronger to prepare me for D-Days #4 and #5 (that happened in 2021). When the race was done, I missed my training times with my paraclete. But change was coming. I was now going to learn more new and different things.

During COVID times, we made silly decisions like everyone else. We bought our dream house (along with two pups– I added this to make you laugh at our stupidity). I wanted a change. To restart life and celebrate what I thought would be *new*. My husband and I went before God. God was all over it. I was so scared to buy this new house, so I begged God for signs. Not sure asking God for signs is biblical, but I did it anyway. He met my request.

We moved forward out of faith in 2020. Child #4 had just left the nest, and only 3 of us were home. Life was good. I was now working part-time, which was something new for our family. I loved my life, being a wife, mom, and mami. But what do you do when the *same* tornado strikes again? Had I not known God wanted us here, I wouldn't have moved across town. I asked God, "Why are we here in this house?" I didn't understand! This was not supposed to happen in my new house, where we were making new memories! God kept impressing my heart, "This is where you will heal completely." I cried and begged God. Even though my foundation and faith were set, everything else had crumbled into a million pieces.

I packed my things and moved downstairs to the guest

bedroom. Here I was in a new house, feeling lost. I now hated my life even though I knew I was supposed to be here. I ended up finding a betrayal trauma therapist, and my husband found a sex addiction counselor. We were navigating a new way of healing. Separately. God and I became inseparable. I made no move without talking to Him. I was learning to be more dependent on Him.

For our entire marriage, my husband and I always went to church. And for the last five years, we prayed a lot together before this all went down. Suddenly, I found myself alone downstairs in this new guest room sharing a bathroom with my 17-year-old daughter. I kept praying.

In 2021, I had 2 D-days: May and December. In May, I filled out the paperwork for divorce. But I never filed. My husband was aware, and he swore he wouldn't hurt me again, which he had said numerous times in the past. In December, he broke my bottom line (a non-negotiable boundary I had). That day (three days before our 33rd anniversary), I drove to the lawyer crying and praying, yet empowered because I had honored my own boundaries. I kept thinking about our wedding day and never thought I'd be doing this. But I knew God had already gone before me.

The staff and my lawyer were soft, gentle, kind, and empathic. I felt loved and cared for. After I filed, the lawyer prayed with me. I knew immediately he was a man of prayer. This man prayed a giant prayer over me. Even I shuttered at his requests and his fear of God. I was about to

GOD OF MY PRAYERS

learn even more about prayer. Every interaction with this man, I was asked to pray about these decisions. He would even share scripture with me to encourage me. He told me to relax and let God work. He shared many miracles he had seen– some of marriages restored, some not. But the changes God made in their lives were miracles. He has dedicated his life to helping others. He was also a pastor– go figure. He became my shepherd. He was there to protect me and empower me by the Holy Spirit.

God became even *more significant* to me as I walked this new road. I had zero clue what I was doing. But God did. God taught me how to stay godly and give Him glory this time. He was my protector. A week later, I barely made it through Christmas. The very next week, I had to tell my kids that I had filed for divorce. God also was with me as I did this. I was so sick and begged God to end my life or my husband's life, so I didn't have to tell my kids. However, this was not God's plan.

Three weeks after Christmas, my husband was served with divorce papers. That night, when I came home from work, I saw my husband crying, drinking, and playing "our" song. It was like goodbye. He was going down south to get help for sex addiction. We both cried and prayed– yes, prayed.

Because I had taken my wedding ring off weeks ago, God impressed upon my heart to get my wedding ring. I wanted to say no to God. But, out of faith, I went and

HEALING STEPS

placed just the band on my finger that night. I said, by faith, to my husband, "Please come back healthy and changed. Please return to fix this mess with me."

He left three days later, and that day, I became the most prominent prayer warrior ever. I'll never forget. It was a cold, winter, snowy day. I said goodbye to my husband, stepped out back on the deck, and told God, "I don't know what you're gonna do, but this is *Your* story." When I came back inside, I fell on my face on the kitchen floor, surrendered my entire family, and prayed for 8 hours straight until my husband arrived down south (which was a battle because he kept threatening to turn the car around or drive off a cliff, which I was okay with at the time). I slept so well that night because praying is exhausting.

From then on, I woke up daily in battle. A battle over everything. The more I prayed, the more Satan fought my mind. I kept saying, "Not today, Satan." I'd walk around the house praying. Praying over my kids, myself, my husband, my decisions, for the car to work, for bills to be paid, for our house payment. Here I am, left in my dream home with my daughter. I planted my feet deep into the roots of God's foundation. I was NOT moving, *nor* was I going to allow Satan to win.

My husband had no idea of my new role—combat wife. The spiritual attacks that happened were not even funny. Things broke, my husband lost his job, we had health issues, my husband got his job back, and crazy things were

GOD OF MY PRAYERS

happening to my kids. Despite all that, God enabled me to do things I didn't know I could. I was making decisions I didn't know I could make! I was scared to death of my situation, yet I was flourishing. I was changing, becoming bolder and braver. I am amazed at how God gives you such power and grace amid a tornado. Prayer continues to grow and change me.

Can you pray? Some days I couldn't. It was reassuring knowing that Jesus went to the throne before we even asked. Sometimes, I would sit on my deck and say, "I know you're praying for me. I don't know what you're saying, but I trust you... sort of." I was too empty to pray. God understands.

As I look at Hannah in 1 Samuel 1-2, I see prayer took a toll on her life. She was so exhausted the priest thought she was drunk! She was desperate and dependent– keeping her focus on the source. She prayed, she watched, and she waited.

I used to think God didn't want me to be pesty. Now, I know God wants me to be pesty. He wants me to talk to Him throughout my entire day. Don't give up asking! Grab your knee pads, get down, and pray! God loves it. It smells good to Him– even the darkest prayers. I know He has all my prayers in a bowl. Yet, I hope never to reread them.

Do you cry out to God? Yell? Maybe write a letter to Him. God can handle anything you say, no matter how you say it! He's big enough.

HEALING STEPS

What are three things you can ask God for right now? How does it make you feel to ask?

Tell Him your needs. Your prayers are a sweet smell to Him.

You are one with Christ.

1 Corinthians 6:17

4

GOD OF MY BATTLEFIELD

I didn't realize my God was a warrior. Over my entire life, I didn't realize that He was calling me to join Him in battle and be a prayer warrior. I was clueless about what this would be like. I will tell you today it's like being a newbie in a boot camp fitness class!

Do you know how often I felt like I had fallen over on the battlefield or lost my weapons? So many times. I wanted to quit and sit and cry. Yet God sat with me.

Do you cry out to God? Yell? God can handle anything you say, no matter how or what you say! The verse that resonated with me, and I spent many days quoting, was, "Greater is He in me, then he that is in the world." 1 John

4:4 (KJV). That verse inspired me to pray with greater boldness. Satan hates prayer. But I knew he couldn't take that away from me. Everything else he was trying to use to destroy me, but he could not destroy my foundation.

God came down to me in my cocoon on my D-day. This reminds me of the Israelites. They were so scared to go up to the mountain where God was. So, He came down. This is so intimate– so precious.

Look at Jesus! He came down and became flesh. What does He still do? He meets me on my deck, in my bedroom and kitchen. He draws near. He made himself known even more to me! I encourage you to stay on your knees; you won't regret it! You will be blessed, no matter how crazy things get! I love seeing how others prayed in the Bible.

As I ask Google, it says Abraham was the first to pray. It seems those in the Old Testament had a different relationship with God. They had audible conversations. Anyone jealous?

They prayed about difficulty– not just for themselves, but for other people. Abraham went to prayer over the lost cities of Sodom and Gomorrah. I couldn't imagine. What do you learn when you read Genesis 18? Moses went to pray for the Israelites. In Genesis 32, Moses intercedes for Israel. Would you have done that? Jeremiah even prayed over Jerusalem. These men of God have such big hearts!

Jeremiah 17:14 has become a prayer I adopted for my

GOD OF MY BATTLEFIELD

own healing "Heal me O God and I will be healed." (NIV). I encourage you to write this out and get it in your heart. Maybe spend time reading Daniel 9. Look at how Daniel prayed and praised. Don't forget to praise.

Is there room for you to be thankful? The Psalms are so full of prayers. The Psalms resonated with me when David asked God to take evil away or my pain away. Can we ask those bold prayers? Yes! Have you found a Psalm that speaks to your heart?

The most precious prayer, I think, is Mary's. A prayer of surrender. It's at the end of Luke 1. It is a beautiful song of prayer, praise, and surrender. She likely was 13 years old. That's so young to pray like that! Put yourself in her shoes. Her reputation was on the line. Our reputation is on the line too. You know how people gossip. She would have been an outcast– possibly a divorced woman. I could be divorced, and I have felt like an outcast numerous times! If I would have been Mary, what would my response have been? What response do you *want* to have? And what response *would* you have? Be honest. Be real.

God wants to show you more of Himself through prayer. We are being changed.

God will fight our battles. This is assured through God being called Jehovah Nissi, which we first see in Genesis 17.

What is your biggest challenge with prayer? Tell God.

HEALING STEPS

God will equip you to join him on the battlefield of your life, family, marriage, and any other circumstance. Get a journal and write/date any requests or miracles. Start keeping track now. Stay curious and stay on your knees.

You are victorious.

2 Corinthians 2:14

5

GOD OF MY BROKEN HEART

I can't remember the year exactly, but I think it was 2016. It was one year past my 3rd D-day. I had chosen to stay in denial (Michelle Mays calls this betrayal blindness), I had become so depressed and hopeless. I had no tools. I was sick of reading my Bible, praying, listening to music. Why was my life falling apart again? I was tired of suffering for "Christ." I wanted out.

But I continued doing all the "right" things despite feeling I deserved a better life by now. I was becoming more and more angry with my husband and God. I was stuck.

I wrote a letter to God, sobbing the whole way through.

Pouring out my heart, I hated it here and was mad at Him. Told Him I didn't want this life anymore, and I didn't want to be His child anymore. I was suicidal and thought it was best to let me go. Hell would be better than living through this pain of betrayal. I told God I didn't even want a heart. A broken heart is so painful– beyond comprehension. I told God I would be hiding my heart, protecting my heart, and *never* be hurt again. Because I believed I didn't have the power to walk away, I asked God to release me. Let me go. Please. My soul wrestled with God over this. I know He is sovereign, and He could release me or not, but would He?

I pictured Him releasing me with an imaginary string tied to my ankle. He was watching me walk away as I waved goodbye to God. (I cry now writing this). I was in such a bad place. I felt so sorry for myself. But I wanted the pain gone so bad—my poor heart. I had to get away from this pain and God. As I said goodbye to God that day, I also said, "I believe in Your keeping power of my soul, and I know in my heart I can't walk away, but I am gonna try. I know You chase people, but please don't chase me. I'm done with You."

My new adventure wasn't as sweet of a time as I had hoped for. But I was in charge now. I went about my daily life without God. I tried hard not to miss Him. I wonder if He saw me. What was *He* thinking? Was He shaking His head? "You poor child." Or was He rolling his eyes at me and waiting patiently? I pretended for a while to be free. Yet I was curious when He would call me back... but praying He wouldn't.

I don't remember how long it had been. But God impressed upon me to write a letter from Him to myself. I started this letter with, "Dear broken child of mine." It continued for three pages. I sobbed as I wrote out words that were impressed upon me for my eyes only. He told me how He understood my pain, and He was using my scars. They would be my gifts. This is the ending below:

> *Please take your heart off the shelf, unwrap it, and return it to me. It's mine. I made it! I will tenderly care for it better than you can. Trust me. You are loved, my child. You're my favorite!*
>
> *Love, Daddy*

This is the first time since 2016 I have read this.

I wrestled with this letter from "Daddy." I felt so loved and seen, but I didn't want to be duped again. I wanted a guarantee never to have my heart broken again!

I responded to my "Daddy" with a six-page letter a month later. I poured out my pain and my fears. I told Him I knew I was believing lies and loved it. I knew I was angry and bitter, but I liked it. I liked having my heart hidden. No one would ever stab it again. I also acknowledged who He was. I told Him I needed repentance and humility.

Here's my ending paragraph of that longer letter:

My blessed Father, God, Creator, Yahweh, Jehovah, Jubilee King, Lamb, Mighty One, Immanuel, and Daddy. You are so awesome, huge, indescribable, yet personable to only me! You know my thoughts, my fears, my desires. You care for me so much that You number my hair. I don't even care about my hair. But You do. You care more about my heart than I do. I want to protect it. You want to mold it. I want to hide it. You want to heal it. I want to let it die, and You want to revive it. I want a fake one, and You want to give me a new one? TRUST YOU, right? Aren't You sick of remaking hearts? Working with the weak? Don't I wear You out? Why do You like messes anyway? That's right... Your glory. You love Your glory. You love it so much that you allow good and evil to happen to get glory. I haven't been giving it. I'm withholding for my self-gain (lie). You have gifted me repentance, but I chose NOT to take it. You have gifted me grace, I denied it;, You have gifted me peace, I chose anxiety. You have gifted me trust, and I choose fear. You are thankful for me, and I choose ingratitude. You have gifted me forgiveness, and I choose bitterness and unforgiveness. You sent your Son to die for all these sins of mine, and I continue to stab Him over and over again on that cross. Yet You tell me to throw my sins on Him, cast! Why? Why did you break His heart for me? Why? It's SO painful; oh, how He hurt for me. He chose to do that. For Your glory!! He was forsaken. The pain must have been awful. Father, I am SO eternally grateful that I will NEVER know your forsaking! EVER! Lord, I throw all these sins at the foot of the cross. Take them back, get them off me. They are making my heart ugly, so very ugly. It's hurting me more than I know to carry this dead heart around. I stink! I need to get rid of it. I have NO clue what You will do with it. NONE. Maybe You won't do anything. But I don't want it. It's up to You what you do with it. You're right, it's Yours anyway! I have been king of my own heart.

Father, forgive me. My arrogance is killing me, killing my marriage, and secretly killing my family. Take my bitterness, anger, hatred, envy, worry, and fears. You know them all. Jesus, thank you for Your death, for dying for these sins, for setting the example of suffering with purpose, focused on the Father's glory. Because of You, Jesus, I can repent, and I can receive forgiveness again and again. I can walk this journey. I will finish. I just can't worry about how. Trust, right? Faith-- one step at a time. Thank you for all these gifts. Especially the gift of knowing You. It's the BEST gift ever! One that humbles me incredibly. Thank you for this journey. You have graciously given me this chapter. I choose to make it to the next chapter. I choose gratitude. I choose repentance. I choose to change with the Spirit's help. To walk forward by Faith.

My view of God changed through that event. He is my Daddy. Do you need to write a long letter to God? What about one from God to you? Wrestle with Him! Make time to do that.

I recommend you listen to the song, "Stars" by Skillet

He sees, He understands, He comforts. He is the God of your broken heart!

You are beloved.

Zephaniah 3:17

6

GOD OF MY FATHER ABRAHAM

Let's look at the book Genesis, where it all began. I am not talking about creation but the Patriarchs. These men of faith. *Wow*, can I just say that I thought my life was messy? I'm convinced these messy men and women of the Bible were put in there to give me *hope*. God does love messes, and God loves to make Himself seen in the midst of them. He loves to fix messes. Take time to read Genesis 12-25. The story of Abraham and Isaac.

So, we all know the story of how Isaac came to be. God had Abraham and Sarah on their journey of trust and faith. God was working on a more extensive plan than I thought. God was teaching them to trust, teaching them to pray. Once Isaac arrived, the teaching continued as Abraham's mess got messier. Now, his mess contains two boys and two jealous women.

Fast forward to when Abraham is asked to sacrifice Isaac. What a crazy idea, God. But God uses it to continue to test Abraham's faith. God then makes Abraham the father of many nations– despite Abraham's continued sinfulness Only God himself is faithful repeatedly. God is a man of His word!

Isaac marries Rebekah, and they have twins. We know Esau sells his birthright to Jacob over food. And Jacob grew up next to his mom in the kitchen. His mom, Rebekah, is deceitful and teaches her son to deceive. Jacob steals the birthright and lies to his dad. How will God fix this? I genuinely feel like my story could fit right in here!

Now, if you have time, read Genesis 26-36. It's a happy story. Shall I mention Leah and Rachel? Precious Leah and God's mercy. God sees and hears her; she was never wanted, yet God uses her to be the mother of Jesus' line. I love this! God is so gracious to use messy people; this gives me hope. In the end, Jacob and Esau are restored. Jacob ends up with 12 sons, as we know. Joseph is the last Patriarch.

Moving onto Genesis 37-50. So much dysfunction. There's jealousy, rage, murder, lies, and more lies that enter the scene. It's a crazy story of how Joseph gets sold, gets a job, and then gets put in jail for attempted adultery (that he didn't do). Then becomes a leader in jail, gets out, and now is working for Pharoah. Is your head spinning like mine?

GOD OF MY FATHER ABRAHAM

How will God fix this? Only God. He shows up in each story. Guess what? He still shows up today in our stories!

What part of God's character do you see here? After reading each passage and each Patriarch? Can you list all the craziness you notice? Is there any that resonate with you? There are so many sexual sins and lies going on. Do you see how sin continues to get worse and how it's passed down? List the consequences you see. Did God ever leave them? Change His mind? When you step back, look at *all* of Genesis. Do you see God weaving a bigger picture? What do you think He is doing? He's mending things!

We are so blessed to be able to look back and see these Godly characters! Real humans with real problems. Today, I genuinely believe some of these characters would be in jail. Do you ever wonder how we would treat them if they were living in today's times? Do you think these guys would be allowed in a church today?

God allows us to look back and see His faithfulness in their lives. We see so much of God's unchanging character that speaks to me today. He is still the same God that I get to talk to! My life is just as crazy as theirs. Abraham and I follow the same God! Looking at the sky, I see the same stars that Abraham saw. There is hope for us because of their lives and stories. Our God is unchanging. How does this make you feel? I get goosebumps. Can you find rest knowing this?

You are God's image.

Genesis 1:27

7

GOD IS MY HANDYMAN

As we look at our unchanging God and the encouragement from the Patriarchs, we see how God still fixes things!

Let's look at the last chapter of their lives.

Abraham– Do you think he learned to trust his God? When you see all the sins involved in Abraham's life, God was still working and used it to bring Him glory. What did God do? He gave them *hope*. "I will bless you with many sons." God gave them a future! God transformed Abraham. He lived an abundant life and passed his faith down to Isaac.

HEALING STEPS

Isaac- Did you know his name means laughter or rejoicing? Do you not love that? This is truly a sense of humor from God! Isaac showed immense faith in getting on the altar to obey his father and God. But God provided a ram in the bush. Isaac was then double blessed with boys. Isaac wasn't the perfect parent, but he had a favorite– Esau. This hairy child grew up knowing how to hunt. I'm sure his father taught him. Esau gave up his birthright and then became so angry with Jacob over it. When they reconciled, they brought each other gifts of peace. Read Genesis 32. It is such a story of hope! Isaac's faith was then passed down.

Jacob– The man who wrestled with God. How brave of him. He was not perfect either. He also married into a totally dysfunctional family. He married two sisters and was blessed with 12 boys. He had a favorite wife and son. The family is torn by jealousy and murder. Now, his favorite wife dies in childbirth. What grief this man has known. But God provides a way for reconciliation with his favorite son and eventually with the whole family. God also provides a way for his family to live throughout the drought. Jacob's faith is then passed down.

Now, let's briefly look at the Matriarchs:

Sarah– What a messy marriage, living with a man who told her to lie twice. And the pain of dealing with the consequences of telling him to sleep with Hagar. She

GOD IS MY HANDYMAN

learned much about waiting on God.

Rebekah- brought deceit into their marriage, and it continued as she helped scheme a lie with Jacob, her favorite child. I wonder if she ever understood all she had done.

Leah- What a messy situation. Leah was chosen to have a child in the line of Christ! But that's not who Jacob loved. There must've been a competition between the two sisters; the jealousy, the comparison. I'll say it: women can be mean. I can't imagine how this household looked. I do know that Leah learned to ask God for *big* things. She knew God. God heard her prayers and answered.

"But God." Do you not love these words? Can you look back over your life and say, "But God?" Make a timeline of your life and divide it into 10-year increments. Do you see God weaving something? Are there any places where you can say "But God" and see how he changed an event in your life for the good?

Where do you need hope today? These characters in the Bible give us such hope. We serve that same God.

"Yet I dare to hope when I remember this: The faithful love of the LORD never ends! His mercies never cease. Great is his faithfulness; his mercies begin afresh each morning. I say, 'The Lord is my portion; therefore, I will hope in him!' The Lord is good to those who depend on

HEALING STEPS

him, to those who search for him. So, it is good to wait quietly for the salvation of the LORD." Lamentations 3:21-26 (NLT)

I went into fix-it mode when I look back at the first D-day. I'll fix myself (get a new hairstyle, lose weight, etc), my family, and my husband over the many painful years. I have learned to say, "You Fix It, God." My experience with God has been my foundation. This foundation has held me firm! God continues to cement my faith (and yours) on top of our foundation—the *Rock*.

Our circumstances may change, but does God? God is *more significant* than our suffering.

Read Psalms 88 - did you find any hope? It's a picture of total despair. Wouldn't you agree? Praise God, we have Jesus and will never be in total despair!

"Because you trusted me, I will give you your life as a reward. I will rescue you and keep you safe. I, the Lord, have spoken" Jeremiah 39:18 (NLT)

He's got this. He's my handyman. He's yours, too.

Do you believe this? What do you need fixing? Make your "honey-do list" for God.

You are a masterpiece.

Ephesians 2:10

8

GOD IS MY SAFETY

Is God safe? Can God be trusted while suffering? As I study the Bible, I know He is. In my situation, I was skeptical. Even the church, men of God, gave me bad advice and left me emotionally hurt. Between church and my husband, I felt everyone was unsafe, including God. Can I trust anyone? Who was safe? HELP!

God is loving, compassionate, and trustworthy... isn't He? When I started having tough conversations with God, I noticed that in the midst of the bad, there were glimmers of hope. I saw God taking care of me in new ways. By answering prayers and even doing miracles. Somedays, I felt like an Israelite in the desert. Loving my consistent manna... then hating manna. Loving God, but missing Egypt. God understood my trauma. I see God was busy helping me feel safe and showing me He is trustworthy. He'd say, "I got this." But at times, I wasn't too sure.

In 2022, while my husband was away getting help for his sex addiction, one of my coaches asked me what I needed for safety. I had no clue. I was safe at home. She elaborated: what *emotional* boundaries did I need for safety? Can I do boundaries? No one has ever suggested it to me before. Is this Biblical?

Let's look at who sought safety in the Bible.

Nehemiah- Nehemiah set clear boundaries when he led the rebuilding of the walls of Jerusalem. Despite facing opposition and distractions, he maintained focus and set boundaries to ensure the successful completion of the project. He was protecting the town from further destruction. (Nehemiah 10:28-29)

Jesus- Jesus consistently established healthy boundaries in His interactions. He set limits with His time and energy, prioritizing rest and solitude to maintain His spiritual well-being. (Luke 5:16). Remember Jesus came to save the world and obey the Father. He never violated this.

Paul- The apostle Paul frequently set boundaries within the early Christian

GOD IS MY SAFETY

communities. He addressed issues of moral conduct, false teachings, and inappropriate behavior. He established guidelines for healthy relationships and communal living.

Moses– Moses set boundaries with the Israelites during their journey in the wilderness. He established rules and guidelines to maintain order, ensure justice, and promote harmony among the people.

Hosea– Hosea set boundaries with Gomer. Trying to keep her safe. Or you could say God set up barriers with Israel.

I needed to understand my core values and how I would honor myself with my values. I also needed to understand what I was capable of. Some days, I could handle more than others. Asking myself what I need and how I feel. Knowing I can say no without guilt. Boundaries were for me. My husband and I each have our boundaries now in all areas of life. To stay whole and healthy. I have learned I can't do everything. To understand what I am capable of or not capable of this week. I am learning to say no. I also have boundaries set for myself that my husband honors, so I feel safe with him. This is helping me rebuild trust with him, due to the many years of destruction. I have over three pages of boundaries that have helped me feel safe.

The categories of boundaries that I need for safety

HEALING STEPS

right now are financial, physical, intellectual, emotional, material, time, sexual, and travel boundaries. I also have bottom lines (non-negotiables). Never to be crossed, or I will leave the relationship. As safety grows in the relationship, we can negotiate boundaries. My bottom lines will never change.

My coach also suggested a therapeutic separation, which she guided us through. We came to agreements as to what it would look like. This also helped rebuild safety.

What are your thoughts on God and being safe? Does God care about your emotional safety? Does God want you in an unsafe situation? What steps can you take to move towards safety? Do you have someone to work with you on boundaries and safety? Were you shocked that people in the Bible have boundaries? I was. Start your list of what you need for safety. God wants us to be safe in all areas of our life. He is the God of safety! He cares so I can rest.

You are God's child.

Romans 15:7

9

GOD IS MY SHEPHERD

Yes, God is my pastor, my shepherd, and my leader. I think. It doesn't feel like it sometimes. Sometimes, I don't want a shepherd. What is a shepherd? A guide, a protector, or someone who cares. Of course, God is all three. Pastors are also called shepherds because that's what they are supposed to do for their church– guide, protect, and care. A shepherd puts their needs last to care for one sheep or the whole flock. A shepherd helps bring guidance and care, whether physically, financially, emotionally, or spiritually.

One main characteristic of a shepherd is commitment to the job. It's demanding and tiring. I know my God is committed, and He never tires. Pastors? Not too sure. Pastors and leaders are humans. Most are not equipped to deal with sex or porn addiction, let alone betrayal trauma

HEALING STEPS

and PTSD. I am thankful that many professionals are now trying to inform the church on how to deal with those issues. It's becoming an epidemic in the church.

The church is an excellent community for holidays, celebrations, sickness, and deaths. It is lacking in resources to take care of addicts and betrayal trauma. Not only in my situation, but I have heard it from many other betrayed women. This grieves me.

Our situation went public in the church. This was so humiliating and traumatizing. I wanted to take my family and run. He was then voted out of two churches over the last 20 years. I know they thought church discipline was the right thing to do, but this was extremely painful for everyone. Addiction hurts everyone. My husband needed help and direction. Our family needed safety and help. I know of other families who were told not to come back to church due to the nature of sin. I know of children of addicts who weren't welcome at a youth group because of their father's sin.

This can cause such a divide. Many women going through betrayal also go through a crisis of faith. We start to question so many things, especially God, and then not being allowed or not feeling safe at church just adds to the loss and grief we already feel. We betrayed partners, already feel so ugly, like a leper– unwanted. So many of us betrayed partners and addicts are left with spiritual abuse instead of spiritual support. I think God is grieved over this.

GOD IS MY SHEPHERD

I am grateful that, while my husband was away getting help, he found a church and a small group to support him. In the meantime, I hid in my house on Sundays. I did visit some churches alone, but the pain was so bad– it was also hard being alone. However, this is where God took the lead and became my one and only Shepherd. I now see how God pulled my husband and me away for a purpose. To teach us each dependence on Him. We could learn directly under Him. We are looking slowly and cautiously for a new safe church community.

Let's look at Jacob, who was a shepherd.

"But Jacob replied, 'You can see, my lord, that some of the children are very young and the flocks and herds have their young, too. If they are driven too hard even for one day, all the animals could die. Please, my lord, go ahead of your servant. We will follow slowly, at a pace that is comfortable for the livestock and children. I will meet you at Seir." Gen 33:13-14 (NLT)

I was a broken, traumatized sheep. So was my husband. We were hurting sheep. My Shepherd waited for me patiently. He was gently leading me, picking me up, carrying me. God urgently directed my husband's steps to be where he would get the care and help he needed. I saw my Shepherd gently caring for all 16 of my family members. He never rushed us but went at our pace. He still does. God knew what we each needed. Jacob understood this. He didn't want to hurt his sheep by rushing it. God paced with me. God is aware and understands that those who are betrayed are paralyzed, numb, and hurting. God slows down. Do I have days where I am tired of this? For sure. Days I don't want a shepherd? Yes. My poor Shepherd has to deal with me as I am fickle; I can't make up my mind. Nonetheless, I know He's committed. He's not going anywhere. I am grateful.

"He will feed his flock like a shepherd. He will carry the lambs in his arms, holding them close to his heart. He will gently lead the mother sheep with their young" Isaiah 40:11 (NLT)

Is this not a beautiful picture? I picture myself snuggled right to my Shepherd's chest. I will receive Him carrying me as a gift.

Where do you see yourself right now? Can you feel your Shepherd's presence? Do you need to be carried right now? You can trust your shepherd's pace. He wants what's best for you.

I want to end with Ezekiel 34:1-10. God gave this to me as I was grieving our church situation. I found so much comfort in it. I love how the Bible talks about even bad shepherds. Ask God to give you the wisdom to establish a boundary if you share your experience with your pastor. Sometimes, pastoral care can serve to make betrayal trauma worse. For example, I didn't have a boundary set. Details of my situation were shared by my pastors publicly before

GOD IS MY SHEPHERD

the church, without my permission.

Now, read verses 11-31. This is all about the good Shepherd. God gave me Ezekiel 34 in the spring of 2022. We may not trust our earthly shepherds, but we can trust our good, heavenly Shepherd. He will take care of us. Follow the right now.

How did reading Ezekiel make you feel? Did you learn anything new? Be encouraged.

You are God's treasure.

Deuteronomy 14:2

10

GOD OF MY CHAOS

"Thanks for the whiplash, God," I said. Just when I thought I knew the plan for going forward, my ride took a sudden turn, and I wondered which way was up. Frankly, I am tired of this chaos. Nonetheless, I keep saying "surrender." Some days, I surrender more easily than others. But yes, I have called God "My Whiplash God." Hang on and buckle up.

When God is with you, you never know what the ride will be. It is chaotic. I have had whiplash so many times that I am starting to expect it. Sometimes, the ride is miraculous; other times it's painful. But it's always a surprise... that's for sure. It's something I never expected. Sometimes, I'll scream happiness at God, sometimes anger. I am learning to wait patiently with God. There are times I just want to get off this roller coaster. I need a break.

Did you know God is a God of chaos? It seems He prefers it. Why would we need God if things were smooth? Does anyone's life in the Bible come to mind when you think of chaos?

I think I could mention someone from each book in the Bible. Maybe I should rephrase the question. Who in the Bible was NOT in chaos?

I decided to ask CHAT GBT Artificial Intelligence:

Those not entangled in direct chaos: Enoch (what a glorious life, how'd he get picked?), Melchizedek (this priest remains a mystery to me. I can't wait to ask him questions in heaven), Joseph (well this proves A.I. doesn't understand chaos to pick this guy), Daniel (in cultural chaos, he brought wisdom and integrity. He was steadfast).

How do I get on this list? That's four people out of hundreds! I don't like chaos. I don't know anyone who does. I prefer lists, plans, and schedules. That's my security. Perhaps it's an idol. So, when the last D-day hit me with full force, I couldn't stay in denial anymore. I felt abandoned, powerless, rejected, and devastated. My schedule, my tomorrow and future, had changed. My perspective changed on life; how I viewed others, my husband, and God.

Chaos is scary. It has no boundaries. It can't be contained. God likes it. He owns it. I was desperate for help, direction, and survival. I wanted safety, peace, stability, and security.

Do you feel you're in chaos right now? Do you believe God is aware of it? What would it look like release this chaos to God?

God understands chaos is scary. He is the master organizer of it. Make a list of what you need right now. Invite God to help. Seek His wisdom. He is sitting next to you in your chaos.

You are sealed.

Ephesians 1:13

11

GOD IS MY DETANGLER

I didn't know it, but my last day of destruction was about to be my rescue. God had enough of watching the same destructive tornado hit our family. I did, too. Our life fell apart, but God was helping it fall into place. God was the only one who knew where the pieces went—my only hope.

God was aware of my husband's two lives. My husband knew my reality. God knew my reality. I was the only one who didn't know my actual reality. My husband was trying to maintain my happy reality and his affair partner's reality. He was also trying hard to keep his secret reality from colliding with mine and my reality from colliding with the A.P. (affair partner) reality.

After each D-day that had happened, my husband became more and more sneakier. He became a better liar. This is the disease of addiction, and this is how it happens. The addiction cycle doesn't go away. It goes deeper and deeper. It took my husband further than he ever wanted to go. Addiction is a *big beast*. The hiding, sneakiness, and lies got more extensive. I was clueless.

But God was NOT clueless. God allowed it to go on for many more years, as this big beast grew more and more. God knew the perfect timing for this tornado. God needed my husband in a specific place and time. He also needed me in a particular place and time. God was setting the stage to crumble it into a billion pieces. God allowed me to see red flags and to question things. God gave me a gut intuition. By faith, I went to my lawyer again. I was being prepped for the storm of a lifetime. I thought the previous storms were big, but the most significant storm was coming. I would soon go face to face with a *big dark beast*.

I felt its presence in our house sometimes. My daughter felt it. I would walk around the house quoting scripture. Three weeks before the last tornado hit again, I received an email from my husband while he was on a plane. He told me he felt confused and told me to pray for him. He felt he was in a demonic hold. This beast didn't want to take its talons out; it had consumed my husband's brain. My husband questioned his own sanity numerous times. He was in the fog of addiction. He would even leave me notes saying, "Please pray." I remained a praying, yet clueless wife.

Meanwhile, God was working on His rescue plan. The weeks before everything came to light, I saw things in my husband that were not him. I knew something had taken over. He was ashamed, hated himself, and was weary of keeping everyone's world from crumbling. The lies he was telling me, the affair partner, and himself. God had a plan. My life was deteriorating rapidly. I was scared and needed out. I filed for divorce, opened my own checking account, and transferred money. I didn't know what my husband was going to do. My mind swirled: Would he leave us? Quit his job? I needed protection.

I was setting myself up for war and was clueless about how to do it. After I filed, I knew something big was coming; I could feel it. This addiction of his was my Goliath. I was terrified– this was so much bigger than me. What has my husband done? I had no clue. I had been praying that God would help me contact the affair partner because I wanted to tell her she was in a web of lies, too.

Through a God-ordained circumstance (and technology), God allowed it. A few weeks before my husband left, God made a way for me to talk to my husband's affair partner. This poor woman needed to hear the truth. She was left dumbfounded and confused. She needed grace, compassion, and truth.

That was the first breaking of this addiction. It was all

coming into the light. The affair partner didn't know God, but by the time I was done talking, I had witnessed to her. I sent her a Bible and many verses on who she is in Christ. I sent her books as well. I still pray for her. May God be gracious and allow her to be in Heaven someday. I pray that my husband's addiction/web of lies does not turn her off to our great God. God had a rescue plan that day, and it may even include this woman. That is how my God works– it's always *more significant* than we think.

Once she was out of the picture, my husband had turned towards recovery and was ready to deal with this addiction. He had completely surrendered to that road and its many consequences. God was slowly rescuing our family from this beast. God was in charge. God was opening so many eyes. We all watched in horror and awe. We all were curious and confused. What would God do now?

Eight weeks into his recovery our precious daughter #4, my rainbow baby, gave birth to her rainbow baby, whom I affectionately refer to as Baby E. Baby E was born on the date her previous sibling went to Heaven. Her middle name means "faithful," so they won't forget how God had been faithful in giving them another child. Isn't this just like our Father? To redeem a date?

My husband flew home from recovery to meet Baby E. My husband and I knew that God had this part of His rescue plan, for Baby E would also be a redemption baby for our story. We were overwhelmed—a nugget of goodness in the

GOD IS MY DETANGLER

destruction of the unknown future ahead. God is so kind and good. Little did we know that 6 months later, more devastation would come as part of another rescue plan for our child #2. She was in need of rescuing. She was living her own double life, two worlds, just like her dad. This beast had been passed down, quietly.

"Wow, God, this is serious."

This broke my heart so badly. When you pray for complete healing. This is what it means— no more lies. I never wondered what else was hiding, but it was there, taking control of child #2. It needed to be brought out into the light. When she confessed her infidelity, my husband and I prayed so hard for her. I was angry that this happened to my daughter. Mama Bear in me was angered. I told Satan to leave my kids alone! All of them. I prayed this addiction would leave, but it wouldn't go away for her until almost a year later. It's hard to be aware of such things.

I wanted to lock her up and keep her safe. But I couldn't. She had a family. They were hurting. Part of God's rescue plan for her was to allow her to conceive a child that was not her husband's. God has recently allowed us the privilege of supporting her and loving on her as she navigates life in this situation. Our whole family now gets an opportunity to love her and take care of her. We get grandchild #7– the number of healing/completion added to our family. Her due date is the same date as I filed for divorce 2 years earlier. God continues to overwhelm me with kindness. Redeeming yet another date.

This Baby K, who was born on his due date, is loved like the other grandchildren. My child #2 is trying to become a healthy adult by getting the help she needs *now*. She is currently receiving her own God stories that amaze me! I remain curious about her situation and her future. I am grateful I can pray for my kids. But God is busy rescuing amid shattered dreams and families.

I am reminded of Judah. (Jacob's and Leah's fourth son) Tamar married his two sons. God saw how wicked they were and intervened and brought death to both sons. This left Tamar widowed twice. She was now "owed" the third son due to levirate law. She was led to believe he would be given to her when he was older. It became apparent that wasn't the case. She proceeds to meet Judah by the city entrance; she had disguised herself, and he assumes she is a prostitute. He then sleeps with her. God restores and blesses Judah with twin boys, and this family of four is listed in Christ's genealogy. This is an amazing mess. For more details, read Genesis 38. But have any of us been so desperate to do this? This woman knew what she was owed according to levirate marriage and went after it. She then became pregnant with twins! Isn't it just like God to give a double blessing. What else does God do? God rescues. How? Well, in this story, God brings Judah back to his family, which seems like a turn of repentance for him. God also grafts Tamar, who may have been a Canaanite woman, into the family of God. This family is also in Jesus' lineage. Check out Matthew 1. *Say what?* That's God's great redemption!

Here's one more story of despair and chaos. Read Genesis 19. Lots' poor daughters had lost their fiancés in Sodom and Gomorrah. It seemed they had no other choice but to have a child. They choose to sleep with their dad. The dysfunction of sleeping with your dad... how awful. But what does God do? These two children turn into two countries, Moab and Ammon. Only God can work such things out.

These chaotic stories about a God who rescues give my story hope. I don't know my ending, my daughter's ending... or my husband's ending. But I do know God will use it. I know it! I believe it! I know He will use yours, too.

Is there a Bible story that is like yours? One that is just as weird? The Bible is full of sexual abuse, adultery, physical abuse, gaslighting, murder, drunkenness, sexual immorality, hypocrites, destruction, lies, betrayal, slaves, and much more wickedness. There's a good chance that one of these will resonate with you in your life or your family line. We can all relate. It's so hard to admit. We have all been touched by sin and dysfunction. It sucks. It almost seems God can't work unless it's crazy and chaotic. It seems like He prefers it. But it's because He becomes *big* when He can show up as the hero and rescue!

We learn how to cling to Him best during hardships. I

HEALING STEPS

love this. I love how He works. He wants a *big* mess. Why? So it can be only Him who gets credit for the detangling! We can point and say, "Wow, look at what God did!" Not what I did. Not the counselor or the church. Only God and God alone!

No one gets credit for my story but God. All my prayer partners can attest to this. Only God could have untangled this mess. My story was like a million pieces of string all knotted together. No one would even attempt to unknot it. No one. My story would have been thrown away had I not taken this mess to the one who has time to untangle it. The one who untangles perfectly. In His perfect time.

Do you believe God can untangle your mess? Draw a picture of your string, and maybe write out all your situations. Give it to God. Allow him to fix it. God will go to great lengths to rescue and get glory from your story. Look how far Jesus traveled for just one demon-possessed man in Mark 5. That's how much God cares! Stay curious and watch how He unravels things. He is the master at detangling.

You are accepted.

Romans 15:7

GOD IS MY DETANGLER

Untangle This....

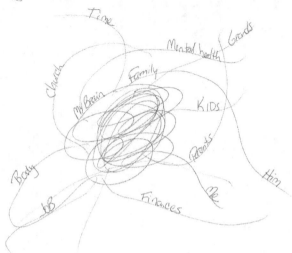

12

GOD OF MY GRIEF

Grief isn't how I pictured it. When I was young, I went to my great grandparent's funeral. There was crying, but I had no idea how long the grief would last. I had no idea there were five stages. I thought grief was only with death! How ignorant I was. I experienced grief with my 1st miscarriage. I grieved alone; I didn't know what was happening or how to share. I hurried myself through the process. I did myself a disservice by hurrying, but there was no helpful advice on grief 20 years ago.

What is grief? A deep, *deep* sorrow of the soul due to a loss. I didn't like grief because it has no rules. I like rules. I wanted to be sad and move on, but sadness kept coming in waves. I felt powerless– just like I felt during betrayal. Grief isn't linear, which also upsets me. How does one do this? I needed someone to tell me how to grieve and be done! I needed to accept the process. The hardest part was trying not to compare my grief with someone else. "Well, she's doing better than me." Grief injures the heart, and trauma injures the brain. The betrayed partner has both injuries. This makes me grieve more.

So many people in the Bible grieved: *Job* is always the first one I think of, then *Jeremiah*– the weeping prophet. *Jesus* wept, and *David* grieved over his son's death.

I know God is near the broken-hearted (Psalm 34:18). My heart was shattered. I was so shattered I didn't know if God could put the pieces back together. As a matter of fact– where were those pieces? It's like my heart died.

I remember falling to the ground when I found out about my husband's affair. "No God!" is all I could scream as I lay there crying and couldn't breathe. My legs gave out. I didn't want this. If only I could go back to yesterday.

God was not shocked by this. He knows it all.

Let us walk through Psalms 69 (NLT) and do some work around this. I love how David has paved the way. Read the verse and notice I have added my thoughts. There is also room for you to add yours. Take your time.

"Save me, O God, for the floodwaters are up to my neck."

Me: *Yes, I am drowning.*

You: _____

_____

_____

_____

> *"Deeper and deeper I sink into the mire; I can't find a foothold. I am in deep water, and the floods overwhelm me."*

Me: *I am drowning in the acid my husband poured on me. I cannot breathe or see.*

You: _____

_____

_____

_____

> *"I am exhausted from crying for help; my throat is parched. My eyes are swollen with weeping, waiting for my God to help me."*

Me: *I am beyond exhausted. My eyes are swollen, my throat hurts from crying and yelling. No one can help me. I am desperate.*

HEALING STEPS

You:_____

_____

_____

_____

*"Those who hate me without cause outnumber the
hairs on my head. Many enemies try to destroy me
with lies, demanding that I give back
what I didn't steal."*

Me: *My husband has destroyed me, us, and the kids.*

You:_____

_____

_____

_____

*"O God, you know how foolish I am; my sins cannot
be hidden from you."*

Me: *I know sin can't stay hidden. I wish it could. I don't
want to know such things.*

You:_____

_____

_____

_____

GOD OF MY GRIEF

"Don't let those who trust in you be ashamed because of me, O Sovereign LORD of Heaven's Armies. Don't let me cause them to be humiliated, O God of Israel."

Me: *Please don't let this discourage others in their walk with you.*

You:_____

_____

_____

_____

"For I endure insults for your sake; humiliation is written all over my face."

Me: *I am so full of shame.*

You:_____

_____

_____

_____

"Even my own brothers pretend they don't know me; they treat me like a stranger."

Me: *Some family members won't acknowledge me; I feel like a leper to everyone.*

HEALING STEPS

You:_____

_____

_____

_____

"Passion for your house has consumed me, and the insults of those who insult you have fallen on me".

Me: *I can't handle anything right now.*

You:_____

_____

_____

_____

"When I weep and fast, they scoff at me."

Me: *Everyone is against me.*

You:_____

_____

_____

_____

"When I dress in burlap to show sorrow, they make fun of me."

Me: *Everyone is staring at me.*
You:_____

_____

_____

_____

> *"I am the favorite topic of town gossip, and all the drunks sing about me."*

Me: *I am the topic at church and family gatherings.*

You:_____

_____

_____

_____

> *"But I keep praying to you, LORD, hoping this time you will show me favor. In your unfailing love, O God, answer my prayer with your sure salvation."*

Me: *Begging for you to get me out.*
You:_____

_____

_____

_____

HEALING STEPS

"Rescue me from the mud; don't let me sink any deeper! Save me from those who hate me and pull me from these deep waters."

Me: *Still begging before I ask for death.*

You:_____

_____

_____

_____

"Don't let the floods overwhelm me, or the deep waters swallow me, or the pit of death devour me.

Me: *Maybe death is better.*

You:_____

_____

_____

_____

"Answer my prayers, O LORD, for your unfailing love is wonderful. Take care of me, for your mercy is so plentiful".

Me: *I know your love and mercy. I ask for more.*

GOD OF MY GRIEF

You:_____

_____

_____

_____

*"Don't hide from your servant; answer me quickly,
for I am in deep trouble!"*

Me: *Help me A.S.A.P. or else.*

You:_____

_____

_____

_____

"Come and redeem me; free me from my enemies."

Me: *Free me, get me out, please.*

You:_____

_____

_____

_____

*"You know of my shame, scorn, and disgrace.
You see all that my enemies are doing."*

HEALING STEPS

Me: *My husband has put so much shame on me. I can't bear it any longer.*

You:_____

_____

_____

_____

"Their insults have broken my heart, and I am in despair. If only one person would show some pity; if only one would turn and comfort me."

Me: *I am in despair- send someone to help!*

You:_____

_____

_____

_____

"But instead, they give me poison for food; they offer me sour wine for my thirst."

Me: *No one cares.*

You:_____

_____

_____

_____

GOD OF MY GRIEF

"Let the bountiful table set before them become a snare and their prosperity become a trap."

Me: *I am having bad thoughts towards my husband of vengeance*

You:_____

_____

_____

_____

"Let their eyes go blind so they cannot see, and make their bodies shake continually."

Me: *This is a good idea- Do It.*

You:_____

_____

_____

_____

"Pour out your fury on them; consume them with your burning anger."

Me: *Yes! Pour a double dose, please.*

HEALING STEPS

You: _____

_____

_____

_____

"Let their homes become desolate,
and their tents be deserted."

Me: *Let him feel this despair.*

You: _____

_____

_____

_____

"To the one you have punished, they add insult to
injury; they add to the pain of those you have hurt."

Me: *Keep it coming*

You: _____

_____

_____

_____

"Pile their sins up high, and don't let them go free."

GOD OF MY GRIEF

Me: *Yes, lock him up.*

You:_____

_____

_____

_____

> *"Erase their names from the Book of Life; don't let*
> *them be counted among the righteous."*

Me: *Wow, this seems cruel. Could I pray this? Give him a*
glimpse of life without You, God.

You:_____

_____

_____

_____

> *"I am suffering and in pain. Rescue me, O God, by*
> *your saving power."*

Me: *Yes, Rescue me from this pain. Stop my heart from*
bleeding.

You:_____

_____

_____

_____

HEALING STEPS

"Then I will praise God's name with singing, and I will honor him with thanksgiving."

Me: *Of course, I will praise you.*

You:_____

_____

_____

_____

"For this will please the LORD more than sacrificing cattle, more than presenting a bull with its horns and hooves."

Me: *I know you love praise.*

You:_____

_____

_____

_____

"The humble will see their God at work and be glad. Let all who seek God's help be encouraged."

Me: *I am seeking help.*

GOD OF MY GRIEF

You:_____

_____

_____

_____

> *"For the LORD hears the cries of the needy: he does not despise his imprisoned people."*

Me: *Hear my cry!*

You:_____

_____

_____

_____

> *"Praise him, O heaven and earth, the seas and all that move in them."*

Me: *I praise you.*

You:_____

_____

_____

_____

> *"For God will save Jerusalem and rebuild the towns of Judah. His people will live there and settle in their own land."*

HEALING STEPS

Me: *What? Will you?*

You:_____

_____

_____

_____

*"The descendants of those who obey him will
inherit the land, and those who love
him will live there in safety."*

Me: *I need safety! Keep me safe.*

You:_____

_____

_____

_____

*How did doing this exercise make you feel?
Even the psalmist feels as we do.*

Grief can't be rushed. Take all the time you need.

You are secure.

2 Corinthians 1:22

13

THE GOD OF MY LOSSES

"'He said,' I came naked from my mother's womb, and I will be naked I leave. The LORD gave me what I had, and the LORD has taken it away, Praise the name of the LORD!" Job 1:21 (NLT)

This is my Sovereign Lord. Who now is the God of my losses. Where there is loss, there is grief. Sin causes our hearts to hurt. I hate loss. It feels so powerless. Did you know that the emotion of loss never comes alone? There are always more emotions to follow. This sucks. My emotions came in droves. My whole being/identity was being changed without permission. Loss and grief are destructive, like a tornado. It has destroyed my heart and soul. It blindsided me so much that I felt I could not even face the future. I couldn't breathe.

HEALING STEPS

The losses I have endured in this destruction make me feel like I need to be in an emotional ICU. I need a hospital for my broken heart.

Here's a list of the losses that I made:

- -The most significant loss was my reality. Past and present. I didn't just lose it- My husband *took it.*
- -Having a faithful husband.
- -Relationships- kids, family, and friends- with you.
- -Loss of Myself- who am I now? Where did I go?
- -My ability to trust.
- -Our finances.
- -My dreams and goals.
- -My marriage.
- -My memories.
- -Our time together.
- -Sleep.
- -My social life.
- -Holidays- all holidays.
- -Daily routines are hard.

THE GOD OF MY LOSSES

- -My capacity to do anything.
- -Mental health.
- -Emotional health.
- -Physical health.
- -Time.
- -Being a present grandparent.
- -Places/hotels/restaurants.
- -SEX.
- -B-days/anniversaries/ holidays.
- -Churches.
- -Ability to love and be loved.
- -Energy.
- -Self-discipline.
- -My family.

Look at the Bible– Job, Naomi, David, Mary, and Jesus.

How did they respond to loss?

Job lost health, wealth, and family. Eventually, his friends, too, didn't understand what he was going through. Job's response was prayer and praise.

Naomi lost her husband and sons. Her response was anger, which rooted into bitterness.

HEALING STEPS

David lost his son and his best friend. Yet he was a man after God's own heart.

Mary lost her son. How heart-wrenching to watch your own son die! God gave her so much strength and grace to endure such a loss.

Jesus chose to lose his own life.

I love how God *pours* compassion, empathy, love, grace, *and* more grace on all of us when we endure such hardships.

Do you feel this way?

Make a list of your losses. Draw a picture of one of your losses. What color do you see your losses in?

What Bible character resonates with you? Ask God right now to protect your heart from bitterness as you acknowledge your losses. Breathe in God's grace. Accept His comfort. Let Him show up for you and provide comfort and care.

Please practice some self-care after listing your losses. It's so hard. Cry, scream, or whatever else. I get it. Learn to allow grief when it comes. Crying can be good for our bodies and refreshing. Acts 3:19– Tears of refreshment.

You are worth a high price.

1 Corinthians 6:19-20

THE GOD OF MY LOSSES

14

GOD OF MY EMOTIONS

As a child, I was only familiar with five emotions my whole life: mad, bad, glad, sad, and fine. It's how I rolled. And I never shared them. *Ever.* Being in recovery has changed that. I am now asked, "How does it make you feel?" to which I respond, "Sad." They say, "Can you go deeper?" Me: "Not really." I didn't want to share because I didn't know how I felt. I never took the time to know what I was feeling. Who has time for this? How did I deal with betrayal trauma? Like anyone else, I'd go in the shower and cry and come out fine. No one needs to know because I *am* fine. *Until* I had a trigger or break down in public, then I would go into a panic because I was out of control again. I was powerless.

When I was first introduced to the feeling wheel,

emotions were new to me. The feeling wheel was overwhelming, and I hated it at first. Now, I find myself using it daily!

I know there are emotions in the Bible. Just read the Psalms. David had so many emotions! God gave us emotions, but I must not have been given many... or so I thought.

Let's look at people's emotions in the Bible:

- David– joy, sorrow, anger, fear
- Job– grief, despair
- Elijah– despair, loneliness
- Hannah– deep sorrow, longing
- Jeremiah– sadness, loneliness, maybe depression
- Jonah– fear, frustration, jealousy
- Mary Magdalene– deep sadness at the cross
- Peter– fear, anger, deep remorse
- Jesus- anger, betrayal, rejection, abandonment, tired, compassionate

When I started to look at how this betrayal trauma made me feel, I had all the horrible feelings. I had to get a feeling wheel to help me know and describe how I felt. I know now emotions are okay as long as I am not controlled by them. Recognizing my emotions has been beneficial, enabling me

GOD OF MY EMOTIONS

to express my feelings when triggered. I am learning to allow emotions to pass through me rather than suppressing them. I now do self-feeling checks at 10 AM and 2 PM to be in tune with my body. This is all new to me. Learning to stay in my reality. Understanding what was true about what was happening to me. What am I feeling? I was learning new words and new feelings!

Shock and denial were the first two emotions I experienced with betrayal. They say shock is a God-given response to protect me. Go figure. Not knowing my next future step made me feel horrified. I was now scared for tomorrow. I felt as if someone had now cut off my oxygen supply, and I didn't know which way was up. I found comfort that God wasn't shocked. He was my refuge and strength, my ever-present help. His wing was there to hold me. He is the God who sees– I can relate to Hagar (my favorite Bible character).

The next emotion was anger. This is a powerful emotion. Anger can be a healthy emotion. In a recent podcast from Seeking Integrity, Debbie McRae explains that "Anger is a protective shield that helps manage betrayal trauma." Anger is rooted in fear. I was, for sure, fearful. One of my therapists suggested making an angry list (I am telling you, too). I wrote out everything I was angry about. I had well over fifty items. I think allowing myself to feel angry and permitting myself to be angry validated me. What my spouse did was awful. Did you know God has anger? Knowing He was also angry at this sin along with me gave me comfort and validated me. Take some time to write a list of all you're angry about.

Months later, I wrote an angry letter and read it to my spouse (that's up to you- when you're ready, with a therapist, please). My list is at the end of the chapter.

Sadness was another emotion that hung on, and I felt like a dark cloud was upon me all the time. Some days, I couldn't quit crying, other days, my tears surprised me. God wept with me. He was near me in my sadness. Someday, I will have no more tears, but right now, I have plenty. And God is keeping them all in a bottle. I am loved. Psalm 56:8.

Then came loneliness. I know God is with me, but man, was I lonely. I needed a human to sit with me and not talk, just sit. When my husband went away for five months to get help, I needed it the most. I was left in our new house with my daughter (who gave me the gift of laughter) and a dog. It got lonely. The bedroom, the garage, the bathroom, and the closet were lonely. This led me to feel lost. Is lost a feeling? At times, I felt like I was a walking zombie, forgetting what I was doing or where I was going. God is with me in the deep waters (Isaiah 43:1-3). He said I wouldn't drown, but I felt that I was. Do you feel lost or overwhelmed? This is where I first experienced the *God of cuddle*. A name for God I gave him. He would hold me close at night in bed while I cried. God has seen my many tears, and I hear Him say, "It's okay."

GOD OF MY EMOTIONS

Another big emotion for me is *shame*. I started having shame for even marrying my husband and building a life together with him. Shame for the times I stayed. Then I started to feel so ruined because of what he did to me. Michelle Mays, in her book *The Betrayal Bind*, refers to it as "Carried" shame. I felt his shame/disgrace was dumped on me after I found out about his sex addiction. This disgrace was a huge heavy black coat that I wore– the same coat I wore on my wedding day. The pain of this disgrace is so heavy and embarrassing. Jesus didn't want me carrying it, but I did it anyway. I felt like an outcast– is that a feeling?

I wrote another letter to my husband and his disgrace. Through that, I returned the disgrace to its proper place. Jesus reminded me I wear a white coat of righteousness (Job 29:14, Is 61:10 Rev 19:8 2). I gave disgrace back to Satan. It's not mine anymore! What a freedom writing that letter was. It is also printed at the end of the chapter. I can now picture myself in Jesus' white robe instead of a coat of shame!

I hate to admit there was a time back in 2007 or 2008 when I was so overwhelmed with emotions, hopelessness, and exhaustion that I felt that I had to end it. I was in despair. I was so scared of myself to have such a thought. I clung closely to my bed on the floor that night, knowing it would all be over if I dared to move. If you have suicidal thoughts, *TELL SOMEONE*. Please get help! Call1(800)273-8255

Empathy was one emotion I needed to learn. Through

HEALING STEPS

the years, my understanding of empathy grew more and more. But going through this and receiving empathy has helped me understand what empathy is and how necessary empathy is when someone goes through any trauma.

Lastly, I learned curiosity. One of the things I say a lot is "Stay curious." I envision myself peeking around the door, waiting to see what God will do next. I stayed in my relationship because I was curious; could he change? I was curious if I could change. I challenge you to stay curious on your journey!

What emotions are most vital right now? What thoughts are coming up right now? What Bible character resonates with you right now? Someday, take time to study the Bible character you chose.

Start jotting down your thoughts on all the anger and disgrace you carry when you're ready. Then, read it.

Did you know God has perfect emotions? He is all emotions perfectly at once!

You are alive.

Ephesians 2:5

GOD OF MY EMOTIONS

Here's my list of things I was angry about:

I am angry at my husband...

- - for lying to me again
- -for sneaking around again
- -for believing you again
- -for convincing me you wanted ME and our marriage
- -for yelling at me Friday night
- -breaking my heart again
- -for not protecting me
- -for not loving me
- -not being intentional
- -for giving up
- -for taking me for granted and all the positives I did to move towards you
- -for drama
- -for being the center of attention
- -for wasted time
- -for violating your own circles and desires and who you want to be
- -for gaslighting me and manipulating me

HEALING STEPS

- -for endangering me
- -for emotional abuse
- -hurting our kids/grands
- -ruining our marriage
- -ruining our friendship
- -for no trust
- -for having no foundation anymore
- -for having a girlfriend while "we" heal

And this is the letter I wrote:

Dear Disgrace and my husband,

I feel stupid because I believed your lies and took you back after numerous other times.

I feel dirty when I think about you being with her more than me.

I feel worthless and broken by emotional abuse and a roller coaster of lies.

I feel undeserving of love because you gave what was mine away.

I feel old, wrinkled, ugly, and fat since you always choose younger women.

GOD OF MY EMOTIONS

*I feel insecure when I think about sex.
Makes me feel used.*

I am not confident because I am broken.

I am a bad wife. Did I not meet your needs?

*I am skeptical since you didn't do what you
said and keep your vows.*

*I feel not valued- low man on the pole. You
preferred time with her and made time with
her.*

*I feel not enough because you search for
someone who may have more to offer: fun,
excitement.*

*I'm embarrassed that our family knows
again.*

*I'm hurt because I feel I was a lousy friend
also, you sought friendship in someone
else.*

*I feel unsafe. You didn't protect me. You
invited her into my life!*

*I feel scared to sleep because you were
building a relationship while I slept.*

*I feel I can't trust myself to make decisions.
I believed you countless times.*

HEALING STEPS

I feel sad you don't have eyes for me and me only.

I'm embarrassed I took you back all those times.

I'm angry to be here again in my new house.

I feel hopeless; your track record sucks.

I feel ungodly for having these issues.

I used to feel attractive and sexy, but now my body doesn't.

I used to care how I looked, but now I don't. Why bother?

I'm embarrassed for all the times I made excuses for you only to know you were with her.

I'm embarrassed I tried so hard to make things work. Disappointed you didn't try hard enough.

I am embarrassed for being vulnerable with you in many forms, only to know you take it for granted.

I am unappreciated for being by your side through thick and thin while you stab me and do things that show me you're ungrateful.

Dear Disgrace, you tried to shame me first with my wedding dress. I took off that black coat of shame, and now you come at me again. I won't have it. It's not who I am, nor is this who I am. I have to give this coat back to you. You did this to me. I won't be destroyed.

Dear Husband, you chose to behave this way. You did this to us, to me, to our family. You ruined all we had. I won't own it anymore. It's not my fault. I will choose to change my perspective and see myself as who I am inside. You won't define me anymore. You take this disgrace and deal with it.

15

GOD OF MY EMOTIONS PART 2

Can Christians be jealous? I was. I didn't want this trauma, yet I had it. My friends seemed to be living their best life. Not me; I was scrambling not to lose my family. They had their family. They were smiling. I was crying, worried, sick, and scared.

I relate to Joseph's brothers, jealous. Life was not fair. I was stuck comparing my life to others. I knew God had a plan, but I questioned if He had one for me.

Oh, how Leah's life resonates with me; she wasn't loved. She wasn't as beautiful or loved as Rachael, but God's plan was for her to carry a child in the line of Christ. She didn't see the whole picture that God was painting. I was left wondering what picture God was painting in my life.

At times, I was jealous of my husband, not of his addiction or consequences, but the fact he was able to get away from his responsibilities while I was home full-time with all my household responsibilities.

In 2021, the feeling of anxiety was unbelievable for me, for now, I felt so much responsibility. I had just started to work 15 hours a week, and since filing for divorce, I was now looking for a full-time job with benefits, a possible new home, and money for the divorce cost. I was getting no sleep, trying to go to therapy twice week, and deciding if I needed to sell the car. The anxiety of all that responsibility was so scary, yet I sat in my destruction, paralyzed to move. I just couldn't right now. It was too overwhelming. Even making a phone call was too much for me. Stress/anxiety can cause so many problems, wouldn't you agree?

I felt apathetic. How on earth do I make myself care about life or God? How many times did I drive around crying, begging God to have someone run into me and kill me? Lord, make it quick! I honestly didn't care. But then I'd remember my sweet children's faces and cry, "What am I doing?" God was with me in the car when I thought about such things. He understands me; I envision him touching my leg and saying, "I love you."

I soon started not to care what I wore or ate– if I ate. I couldn't get to church sometimes; who wants to see

GOD OF MY EMOTIONS PART 2

people? I had God and my Bible. And guess what? He met me in my room! He didn't want me to pretend anyway, which I was used to doing. Guess who else was apathetic in the Bible? Did you know Jonah is sometimes called the Apathetic Prophet? He didn't want any responsibilities. I can't tell you how much I relate to that man, and at times, I am jealous he got three days in a whale alone!

I love how God gives such deep grace that it extends to a crisis. He's too kind to me. The fact I am still upright in this destruction is pure grace. This sucks, and I've had to learn to give myself grace daily. Yep, I'm not able to do laundry today. It's okay that I'm crying again. It's okay that I can't get dressed. It's okay that I can't think or work; it's okay to take care of myself. It's all in God's grace. He had dumped buckets on me, and I pictured myself swimming in grace. Oh, to drown in grace. Please don't stop pouring out grace on me.

The most challenging and biggest emotion that I hate is *vulnerability*. No, thanks. The thought of vulnerability made me cringe. I learned to say "I am fine" before I realized someone asked me how I am. Have you seen how people look at you if you say you're not okay? My therapist keeps saying I have to learn vulnerability. She has taught me, and I am learning! It's been hard, but others have blessed me when I share my needs, tears, and feelings. I am seeing my lack of vulnerability has caused a lot of issues, especially with myself. I honestly didn't even understand myself. I am learning to ask myself, "How am I?" "Do I have any needs

HEALING STEPS

today?" It's been good to voice them without expectations to have them met. Understanding my needs and how I feel has helped me better understand myself.

To me, having needs used to mean I wasn't not good enough. How could I be perfect if I had needs? Previously, I believed that being independent meant I couldn't show my emotions to anyone, so I kept them hidden. Embracing authenticity with myself and others has been integral to my personal transformation.

What emotion is the hardest right now for you? Take a look at the feeling wheel.

I love how Jesus was so vulnerable with his friends and his God. He shared emotions: anger, weeping, fear. He told His father. I told my Father God also. He met me right where I was. He held me and sat with me.

Have you tried to share your emotions with God? Can you? Try a journal.

God listens. God understands. He made you.

You are redeemed.

Ephesians 1:7

16

GOD IS MY COMFORT

"In his kindness God called you to share in his eternal glory by means of Christ Jesus. So after you have suffered a little while, he will restore, support, and strengthen you, and he will place you on a firm foundation." 1 Peter 5:1 (NLT)

"Think about the things of heaven, not the things of earth. For you died to this life, and your real life is hidden with Christ in God. And when Christ, who is your life, is revealed to the whole world, you will share in all his glory." Colossians 3:2-4 (NLT)

"So we don't look at the troubles we can see now; rather, we fix our gaze on things that cannot be seen. For the things we see now will soon be gone, but the things we cannot see will last forever." 2 Corinthians 4:18 (NLT)

HEALING STEPS

I don't know about you, but for me, it's so easy to turn my gaze somewhere else. So many people and things seem to call for me to focus on them, not Him. But I believe it's possible to see Jesus in every aspect of life if I can fix my eyes on Him and the fruit of His Spirit. How do you feel when you read these verses? What thoughts do you have?

For me, at first, these verses didn't help me. People would say these verses to me or send them to me. I'd appreciate them, but all I could think about was I wanted this suffering gone *now*. I didn't want to think about heaven or any more tears. I could barely stand up. How could I focus on myself? I didn't know what was real or not. Was this temporary? Was this a joke? Where was Jesus? I knew He was in this debris, but where? How dare He allow this!

Let's switch gears. Do you ever ask yourself how God allowed His son to die? His son suffered, I know, but I don't want to suffer. Jesus is God; I am not. Jesus was abandoned when God turned his back while He was on the cross. Oh, how I relate to the feeling of being abandoned. I could cry now.

I know Jesus focused on God's will, eternity, and love for us while suffering. Yes, focusing on the right things can help with suffering. But sometimes suffering just sucks!

I feel bad for Jesus. Who comforted him in the garden? His disciples were sleeping. Did Jesus feel betrayed they were sleeping? His friends and family let him down. How

GOD IS MY COMFORT

lonely is that? His Father comforted him while He prayed. And yet, now He is about to be abandoned again, this time by the Father. This makes my heart hurt. I understand this! I hate understanding this, yet I am privileged to understand. I am grateful God will never abandon me.

Who has been betrayed in the Bible? Let's look:

- Delilah betrayed Samson numerous times.

- Joseph's brothers agreed to betray Joseph and their father. How horrible to have a family member do this to you!

- Absalom betrayed King David, his father. The shock must have been devastating.

- The most famous betrayal of all is Judas betraying Jesus. A close friend. Oh, the hurt Jesus and the disciples must have felt. Their close circle was violated.

Betrayal and abandonment are common themes in the Bible. Why had I not understood this or seen it? Because I wasn't aware of it yet. Now, I read the Bible with skeptical eyes. I don't trust anyone in there. Watch out; even the seemingly best characters will mess up.

Where there is betrayal, there is no trust. No safety. But God says, "I am here. I can bring you comfort and safety when others hurt you."

Praise be to the God and Father of our Lord

HEALING STEPS

Jesus Christ, the Father of compassion and the God of all comfort, who comforts us in all our troubles, so that we can comfort those in any trouble with the comfort we ourselves receive from God. For just as we share abundantly in the sufferings of Christ, so also our comfort abounds through Christ.

2 Corinthians 1: 3-5 (NLT)

Do you believe God can bring you comfort? I picture him empathizing with me and understanding me. What do you imagine? Do you think God comforted Jesus? Where are you seeing God's comfort right now? Ponder this and write freely.

Will you let God comfort you? In what ways has He comforted you? I have seen God quiet my soul with nature, perhaps a human hug, or a gift I received, a listening ear or a Bible verse that I came across. Look for God's comfort. Stay curious.

You are a citizen of heaven.

Philippians 3:20

17

GOD OF MY DARES

In 2001, when my life was first destroyed by betrayal, I felt powerless, hopeless, and helpless. All I could say was, "I surrender to whatever you want, God. Show me what to do, God!" I was trying to cry and suffer for Christ. There wasn't help for my trauma 20 years ago. I only knew to hide, cry in secret, and pull myself up by my bootstraps alone.

Even amid all the betrayal behind my back, my love for my husband continued to grow over the years. He has so many great qualities. My husband still did nice things for me; we always dated or did overnights. As the kids got older, we made weekend trips and week-long getaways. We shared many hobbies: running, shopping, biking, and hiking. We took the kids on vacations. Although he had difficulty being present, I can now look back and understand why he acted that way. But I knew in my heart he loved me.

When I had talked with some of the other past affair partners, I told them, "He loves me." One even validated it and said, "I know he loves you." I understood they were his chemical soup, but I was his love– his *wife*. We had children and grandchildren. We grew up together, and I have a history with him. We went through the good, bad, and ugly for 33 years. The other partners had the gross, ugly, lying, make-believe world with him. So, when this last event occurred (2021), I had heard him on the phone with "her." My heart and boundary were broken, so I secretly filed for divorce.

Yet, I begged God to take this from me! I demanded God fix this problem. I believed He would. This time, though, I was done surrendering. I would now stand up to God and remind Him who He was and what I wanted. I wanted a new husband and marriage. I remember standing on my deck in the snow and freezing temps, telling God to act *now*. I rehearsed to Him how capable He is. How He still does miracles and how I need miracles *now*. I would not relent. That's where my prayer and fasting took even more form. I was not going to surrender to my husband's behavior. I have learned over many years with myself that I am a fighter, a warrior. Surrender wasn't going to happen anytime soon.

The ironic thing is, I saw for the first time my husband surrender; he surrendered to whatever consequences that

GOD OF MY DARES

happened. He surrendered to the divorce and to whatever I asked. He surrendered to my boundaries; he surrendered his job and his family. He said he wanted whatever I needed. I could take everything and anything. There was no fight in him anymore.

This was a considerable change. I was challenging God to clean up this mess. To fix my husband, myself, and my marriage. I was still moving forward with divorce *and* still praying like crazy for a miracle. Seeing my husband surrender and say whatever to God made me question if it was real or if God was tricking me.

I felt God say in my heart, "Do you challenge me?" Going toe to toe with God has helped my faith, for I have stayed curious and been in awe of what my God can do. I wouldn't leave God alone. I was so pesty. I did not give up! This led my husband to be curious. He was doing his own praying. He owned all responsibility for what happened and accepted the consequences. He said he supported and respected whatever I needed to do. He wouldn't even get a lawyer to fight against me. This was a significant change. That could only come from a big God.

Let's look at a few people who dared to dare God to move!

- Read Exodus 32:9-14. Moses pleads for the Israelites. What love Moses has for these people! What does God tell Moses? How does Moses respond?

HEALING STEPS

You see, Moses didn't want to be on this journey. When God calls him, he talks back to God; he doesn't just obey immediately. He has an excuse and says, "I can't speak." God is aware of this, and God uses Moses in unique ways in the journey.

- Read Genesis 18:18-62. Abraham pleads with God not to destroy Sodom. It's like they have a deal going on. I would have loved to hear them interact.

- How did it end? Read Genesis 19

- In John 2:1-12 Jesus says, "My time has not yet come." But Mary tells the servants to listen to Jesus anyway. She trusted Jesus because she knew Jesus was capable of turning water into wine.

I can relate to Mary. She had faith and boldness to give the servants to Jesus even though He said His time wasn't here yet.

- Read 2 Kings 20:1-11- King Hezekiah doesn't accept his fate– He presented his request along with his tears! God gives him 15 more years of life because of this!

Did you notice Hezekiah asked for a sign? A big sign.

He knew His God and what God could do. Does this challenge you?

Is there something in your heart that you want to

challenge God with? Bring it before Him and keep persisting. Be bold and courageous. Allow Him to change you as He builds your faith muscle.

You are not a slave to fear *but* to righteousness.

Romans 8:15

18

GOD OF MY GARDEN

Do you like to garden? I don't. I don't know anything about flowers or veggie gardens. I can barely keep flowers alive when my husband brings them home– even though I love flowers! When we bought our house in 2020, it was loaded with beautiful flower gardens. Little did I know the work that would need to be done in the fall and spring. Who has time for this? It was very overwhelming. To this day, whenever I see a plant, I question if it is a weed or a flower.

I found out last week as I was pulling what I thought was a weed that it was a beautiful ground cover plant. Thank you, Google Lens for revealing that to me. I am reminded God is my gardener. His gardening skills are outstanding. He knows how to take care of me. This world and creation were His ideas. The soil, bushes, flowers, and weeds are all part of His design. I have friends and family who garden. They love gardens and taking care of them. They tell me about the value of the particular ways you are supposed to garden. I am shocked at how much there is to know!

I started thinking, my body is a garden. How do I take care of it? How am I treating it? Am I nourishing it? I can ask myself about all the realms of my body: physical, spiritual, emotional, and sexual. It's all part of my body. My garden. God knows me and my garden. He made me!

What part of your garden is doing well? What needs improvement? Rate yourself 1-10 on these categories:

- Physically -

- Emotionally -

- Spiritually -

- Sexually –

For me, during betrayal trauma, these are my answers:

- Physically - 2/10. The first thing I did was understand how to get the sleep I needed, then the nourishment I needed, and then exercise.

- Emotionally - 0/10. I found a betrayal trauma therapist right away.

- Spiritually - 8/10. I ensured I stayed in God's word and called on prayer partners for help and prayer.

GOD OF MY GARDEN

- Sexually - 3/10. Because of the sex injury that happens due to betrayal, I went on a journey to understand my body– learning to like and accept my body from head to toe, accepting and loving the way I am made.

Read Isaiah 64:8 - What character qualities do you see in God here?

Read Jeremiah 18:1-10 - What qualities of God do you see here?

Read Isaiah 41:25 - What do you think of when you read "Tend to the clay"? Do you feel tended to?

God is the ultimate Potter. He knows a lot about art and clay and gardening!

When I think of gardening, I think of the verse about pruning, John 15:2. How does this verse make you feel?

Who wants to be pruned? Not me, but please prune my spouse.

Little did I know that while God was working on my spouse, He would also work on me. Whether I wanted it or not.

The Master Gardener was gentle with me. I needed nurturing. God knew. He was well aware of my needs. He was compassionate, patient, and gentle. He knew I was like a fragile flower, and if the slightest wind blew, I would topple over to my death. He knew whether I needed shade,

HEALING STEPS

rain, or sun. He had my back. Looking back, I see provisions in multiple ways: through laughter, friends, finances– even through gifts of my favorite food, popcorn! This is all part of him taking care of me. It makes me feel so loved when I remember my blessings. Another method through which God has refined me was by nurturing empathy, endurance, reliance, perseverance, steadfastness, and confidence within me. He was actively shaping me to reflect the image of His Son.

What Bible character do you think of when you think of gardening and God pruning? Weren't they all molded and shaped into the likeness of God? By God's grace, they all reached the finish line and died closer to God than they started. By His grace, I will, too!

Look up Job 23:10. What are your thoughts? God knew my future; He is refining me into gold, and the process can be excruciating.

In recovery, everyone says, "Trust the process." I hear this echoed with God. He says, "Trust My process." He knows this is painful, but He is gentle. Trust His timing, guidance, and wisdom.

Which area are you having a hard time trusting God right now? Whichever area it is, that's okay. It's normal to be frightened. List your emotions right now. Then, tell yourself it's okay to feel this way.

Draw a picture of a garden or a flower. Now color it.

Why did you choose that color? How does this picture make you feel? Write your name on that flower.

Do you see how beautiful you are? God does.

You are a branch.

John 15:15

19

GOD OF MY BODY.

My body went through so many changes as I grieved. The brain fog is real. I frequently misplaced my keys or glasses. I couldn't cook or do laundry and never made the bed. I desired normalcy but failed miserably. Simple things were now so overwhelming to me. People would say something, and I couldn't hear it or understand it. Remember how Charlie Brown's teacher sounded? That's what I heard. The kids would say, "Mom, we just told you that." I would often yell at myself, "Why can't you put things back where they belong?" "Where are my shoes?" Jesus is our helper, and boy, did I need help. (Psalm 46:1, NLT) "God is our refuge and strength. Always ready to help in times of trouble." Okay, God, please help.

Grief is exhausting. It wreaks havoc on your body. David knew distress, grief, and body aches. We see this in

Psalm 38. I can relate to this passage and the suffering.

For me, my body was losing hair. I was losing my appetite, getting no sleep, and having many trauma-induced symptoms. (see appendix for list) I barely could do one thing at a time. I had to remind myself to be C.A.L.M:

C - Center yourself. Take deep breaths.

A - Assure yourself. Remind yourself of who you are. You are brave.

L – be Level-headed. How's your thinking? Any cognitive distortions?

M – use Mindfulness or Meditate. Read some scripture, listen to a song, or find a mantra.

These tools are used to help you ground yourself. Be present with yourself, breathe slowly, rehearse what is true, and assure yourself who you are. It's mindset work. You will be okay.

I've learned when I'm in such a heightened, hyper-vigilant state of trauma that self-care is beneficial. Why is it important? Because we are giving ourselves oxygen first before we help others. It helps us to make it through the day.

When I first found out about my husband's unfaithfulness (2001), I was homeschooling three out of four kids. I had no time for self-care and thought that it would be highly

GOD OF MY BODY.

selfish if I did. I have realized it's now my number one item to do daily. I ask myself what I need today. Self-care can be saying no or saying yes. I think sitting on my deck alone for 10 minutes is self-care. I had to learn about myself and my needs. I had to learn to schedule self-care. If this is hard for you, make it a goal to do at least one thing for yourself daily. I have provided ideas at the end of the book.

Make sure you prioritize your sleep. You can't heal without it. Talk to your doctor if you need help. Sleep helps heal our brain! God doesn't sleep, so we can rest peacefully knowing He keeps track of things for us.

Here are some verses that helped me stay C.A.L.M: Psalms 3:5, 4:8,127:2, Proverbs 3:24, and 1 Peter 5:7.

What are your thoughts on these verses? Write them out on cards and keep them near.

> *I look up to the mountains- does my help come from there? My help comes from the LORD, who made heaven and earth! He will not let you stumble; the one who watches over you will not slumber. Indeed, he who watches over Israel never slumbers or sleeps. The LORD stands beside you as your protective shade. The sun will not harm you by day, nor the mood at night. The LORD keeps you from all harm and watches over your life. The LORD keeps watch over you as you come and go, both now and forevermore.*
>
> **Psalm 121 (NLT)**

This is so reassuring! God's got this!

Over the last 33 years, I have had 9 STD tests. They were all horrific. I hate my medical record, it makes me feel embarrassed, gross, ugly, and angry. I am scared of what the doctors or nurses will think.

It made me so angry! In 2021, I learned I needed a new perspective; I was going to take care of my body. I would view it as a gift. It was going to be my self-care. So, I walked in and said, "For my self-care today, I'd like an STD test just to make sure I am still clear." My tone and perspective were different. I was proud to care for myself and this body God gave me. I was brave that day, as God was beside me the whole time.

I recently went back to the doctor for a physical and broke down. It's still triggering for me to be in her office. God gets it. He's there. Remember to take care of yourself! God has given us doctors to help physically, emotionally, and mentally.

One more thing about your body is that when we go through betrayal trauma, we all go through a phase where we hate our physical bodies. We wonder what's wrong with us, and then the criticism starts in our heads. I'm not tall enough, young enough, or pretty enough. I even went through a hair coloring phase because I was trying to improve my outer image. We may lose or gain weight. We must learn to be gentle and kind to ourselves. Learning

GOD OF MY BODY.

to love yourself is hard. Learning to love your body is complex; give yourself grace.

As I walked this journey, I read a book about the female body. During that time, God also made it known to me it was time to deal with some childhood sexual trauma. As a teenager, I had my breasts touched twice without my permission. The situation was so traumatic for me that I took ownership and blamed my breasts. During this journey, I learned I wasn't at fault! I was the victim.

I had so much shame about my breasts for so many years. My breasts have always been small, and I liked it like that! As I grew to love my body and worked on my shame, God started showing me how to love my breasts. I started to pay attention to my breasts, putting lotion on them and my whole body, caring for them like I did for the rest of my body. Guess what? They grew.

I am not joking. I wish I were. I am still laughing at God about this! My close friends and kids notice. I am embarrassed! My therapist said that my breasts were finally able to be what they were meant to be. But as for my new size, I am still not too sure. I had to buy new shirts and bras. I am once again trying to love my new body.

How's your body? How do you feel about your body that God made? Do you need to schedule an appointment or bloodwork for self-care?

I recently listened to a podcast on reclaiming your

HEALING STEPS

body image after betrayal trauma. Here are my notes:

1 - Identify your negative self-talk. "Am I enough?" Yes, you are enough. God made us enough.

Challenge: Would you want your children talking to themselves the way you're talking to yourself?

2 - Look at your *whole* self. You're more than a body, you're a daughter, a mother, a grandma, an aunt, a friend, a sister, a child of God. See yourself as a unique soul.

3 - Give thanks for your body: What has your body done for you? You can walk, eat, talk, hear, think, have periods, and have children. Cherish it. Try to remove anything in your life that causes you to compare yourself or cause negative talk. Surround yourself with positive, vulnerable, trustworthy people. Do something nice for yourself. Make a list of all your non-physical traits and celebrate them.

Your Father made you special. Can you give thanks?

You are His.

Isaiah 43:1

20

GOD OF MY SANITY (AND INSANITY)

"Listen, O Israel: The LORD is our God, the LORD alone. And you must love the LORD your God with all your heart, all your soul, and all your strength. Deuteronomy 6:4-5 (NLT)

This is so impossible. Yet we are called to do it. How does one do this, especially while in devastation? God gives us grace and strength as we go through troubles. We need to get control of our minds, even though the trauma has caused such brain fog. I needed help with my focus to get my strength.

> *Don't worry about anything; instead, pray about everything. Tell God what you need, and thank him for all he has done. Then you*

HEALING STEPS

will experience God's peace, which exceeds anything we can understand. His peace will guard your hearts and minds as you live in Christ Jesus.

Philippians 4:6-8 (NLT)

Another impossible verse, especially when you are feeling so overwhelmed. It is a great idea not to be anxious, but hard to do. But where was my mind? My mind was devastated; I had such fear of my future. I kept picturing the horrendous things that were revealed to me. It consumed me with thoughts of my old life. I had so much anxiety as I walked this unknown road.

My mind would get away from me and leave me feeling even worse. I was tossing and turning at night, having bad dreams. I read on a website somewhere to allow myself 3-5 seconds to think of a wrong thought and then say, "That's enough." That's so hard to do! I get why they suggest that. It's not healthy to dwell on the negative. I was told to think of good things and quoted the above verse, but no one would tell me *how*. How can I switch my mindset? Sometimes, I wish God's word would be more specific. I needed details to help me.

God did provide a good therapist who helped me with ideas for my mind. For the past few years, I have been doing a gratitude journal. I started with three gratitudes a day. Some days, I couldn't even come up with three.

Write three things about who you are. Either your

GOD OF MY SANITY (AND INSANITY)

character or who you are in Christ. This is so good to do because we feel destroyed and broken when we sit in destruction. But who are we? Take a deep look. Your character was not destroyed, even though it feels like it. Who does God say you are?

Lastly, list three things you are grateful for. It doesn't have to be big.

Another thing that can help speak truth and gratitude over you is music. Especially when you feel insane. The Bible mentions people who felt insane. I believe that King Saul almost lost his mind and was overwhelmed by the despair he felt in his depression. He found music to help calm him. Does music help you? Worship music helps me get focused, but to be honest, if you came to visit me, I'd be playing 70s-80s music.

King Nebuchadnezzar II was a powerful king who went mental and lost his mind. He lived seven years as an outcast, ate grass, and became unrecognizable; it even talks about his fingernails resembling claws. He was insane.

When my husband was at the deepest part of this sex addiction, he became someone I didn't recognize. I kept saying to him, "This isn't you." "Where'd my husband go?" I was watching his mind change. He shared with me that he felt oppressed sometimes. He was scared. He would pray for help. He told me he was going insane and didn't know how to stop it. I didn't know what was happening but prayed hard for deliverance. We were both scared. He was rising to the top at work, yet I was watching him crumble inside.

Having two worlds would make anyone insane. After I filed for divorce, I knew my husband was going to be losing it all. Two weeks later, he chose to turn and get the much-needed help. We were both so scared. His life was crashing; he was *not* on top anymore. He had everything: wife, kids, job. It was all going to be gone soon. *All*. I told him and others, "I feel I am watching 'King Nebuchadnezzar fall.'" God was stripping him of everything, and God was working.

I love what God did for King Nebuchadnezzar:

> *When my sanity returned to me, so did my honor and glory and kingdom. My advisors and nobles sought me out, and I was restored as head of my kingdom, with even greater power than before. Now, I, Nebuchadnezzar, praise and glorify and honor the King of heaven. All his acts are just and true, and he is able to humble the proud.*
> **Daniel 4:36-37 (NLT)**

Sin makes you insane. It took seven years, and King Nebuchadnezzar repented. Repentance takes time; sometimes, it is immediately. But not always. For our story, my husband started seeing a therapist six months before I filed. I believe the desire for repentance was there, but the

GOD OF MY SANITY (AND INSANITY)

compulsive sexual behavior still had such a hold on his life. This is addiction; the sin doesn't just go away. Could God cause a once-and-done change? Yes! But, for my husband's story, it would not be that pretty. He was seeking help and was still addicted. He wasn't desperate enough; he couldn't get out yet. Sin continued to make him crazy. He hated his sin; he did want out. Only God knew how to do this.

We didn't understand addiction and the compulsion. He was about to lose everything; he was depressed. Another turn from sin happened again in January 2022, when he left that morning to get the help he needed. God was slowly helping him do a 180 turn but in 10 degree turns instead. God was gentle and patient with my husband. He knew what my husband needed.

God knew how bad things were. God knew my husband needed gentleness, mercy, and love. He knew how fragile his mind was. God met my husband right where he was. God brings repentance differently to people. God has the most patience. He was giving my husband time. He allowed his mind to come back slowly; God was the only one who knew how bad my husband was. The rest of us remained clueless.

After my husband arrived at the sober living house, I talked to the coach at the place where my husband went. The coach said, "He's really bad." I was shocked; my husband kept it all hidden. But God knew. God provided rest, healing, and total repentance. Seventeen days after he

HEALING STEPS

arrived to get help, the final turn of repentance happened. God slowly, gently opened my husband's eyes. God is a kind, patient, loving shepherd. God isn't in a hurry. He was doing a slow, deep work on my husband to give complete healing.

We expect immediate change. God wanted a complete, true change. God is the surgeon. Now healing could start, which would take years. I believe, in time, God will heal my husband completely. I had to learn not to expect such immediate change. Repentance was here. It was slow, hard, and painful– yet good. My husband was like King Nebuchadnezzar. Could God restore his sanity? Could God restore *my* sanity?

Because this destruction was causing me to lose my mind, I remember at one point I felt so defeated by my brain that I asked my husband if I needed to go to the psych ward. God understands. He saw my insanity. He restored it between music, prayer, and His Word. God can restore your sanity, too. It takes time. Be patient with yourself. Cry out to Him for help. What thoughts do you need to confess and take captive? Ask God to help you control your mind. And list some ways God has provided for you at this moment.

How has He been good to you today?

Don't copy the behavior and customs of this world, but let God transform you into a new person by changing the way you think. Then

GOD OF MY SANITY (AND INSANITY)

you will learn to know God's will for you,
which is good and pleasing and perfect.

Romans 12:2 (NLT)

What truth about God do you need to remind yourself? There were days while crying that I had to keep reminding myself of God's goodness. And to "Not depend on [my] own understanding" (Proverbs 3:5, NLT) over and over again.

Find a time daily where you can sit and journal.

You are free.

Romans 6:14-18

Check out the Appendix page for recommended journals.

21

GOD OF MY LAUGHTER

How can one think about laughing while in the middle of such devastation? It took me a good long while to smile, let alone laugh. I learned that taking care of myself and going places I enjoy made me smile. But smiling in the middle of grief is truly hard. It's nearly impossible. That's okay, though– there's no rush. Joy comes in the morning. But when would morning come?

Does God laugh? Of course not; He is just and holy, right? Why would He laugh? Being a firstborn, I didn't laugh much. I was a serious, stiff, rule follower, so that's how I pictured God. Making rules we must follow, or we die. It caused so much self-righteousness in me. I started to think I would have obeyed much better than those in the Bible; I would have been a phenomenal pharisee! I tell people now I am a recovering "elder brother," like the one

HEALING STEPS

in the parable of the prodigal son. The point is, it was not fun to lack joy.

I married a fun man. But I was not a fun wife or mom. I was known as the "downer fairy." I couldn't dream; I just stayed in reality. Who had time to dream? There were too many rules to follow. I majorly regret this. Raising a big family, I was in drill sergeant mode, and I did a darn good job. But I'd love a do-over. Going through this betrayal process has taught me to let loose, calm down, and breathe grace. I started to see laughter and participated in it. I looked for silly, fun things– like dancing in the kitchen. Trust me, my kids noticed! I started to notice funny things that God would bring my way. A silly animal or a crazy idea.

My heart softened towards empathy and grace after many betrayals and sadness. Our 5th child arrived in 2004, full of life; her middle name is Joy. I was changing, and this child has brought me much laughter; I wish I could be her. She is so goofy and doesn't care who is watching. I have learned to laugh so hard with her that I have almost wet myself (numerous times). I watch her with her siblings, who are always dying of laughter with her.

Looking back at old photos of all my kids, I see many things to laugh about. I hear the silly stories of their childhood, and we all laugh. It's so freeing to laugh– gut-belly laugh. I had missed out. And now God has given me grandkids to make me laugh. *I* am now the goofy dancing one.

I have realized as part of my healing, I need laughter. I

need comedy now before bed to relax. I have even started to buy tickets to see comedians. We all need laughter. I am convinced God gave us laughter. He knows we need laughter and loves it when we enjoy his provisions. Laughing even calms the nervous system!

Laughter is vulnerable, which I never experienced until recently. Laughter is contagious. People want to laugh, yet sometimes I think we are scared of it. Can Christians laugh? Is there a rule about it? No, there's not. So don't be afraid!

The God of the Bible is depicted as having emotions, including the ability to laugh. I know the Bible portrays God's serious nature, such as holiness, justice, and love. But there are instances where God's laughter is mentioned. It's mentioned in Psalm 2:4 and Proverbs 1:26.

Let's take a look at a few Bible characters:

Sarah: In the book of Genesis, Sarah, Abraham's wife, laughed when she overheard the angel of the Lord telling Abraham that she would conceive a child in her old age. First, Sarah's laughter was disbelief, as she considered herself too old to bear a child. However, her laughter turned to joy when she gave birth to Isaac, fulfilling God's promise.

Isaac: The name "Isaac" itself means "laughter." His birth resulted from God's promise to Abraham and Sarah. His name was given because of Sarah's laughter. Isaac's laughter is not explicitly mentioned in the Bible, but the connection between his name and Sarah's laughter is significant.

HEALING STEPS

Job: God restored laughter and joy to Job in due time. Isn't it just like our God? Job 8:21

Hannah: In the book of 1 Samuel, Hannah, the mother of the prophet Samuel, offered a prayer of thanksgiving to God after she conceived and gave birth to her son. "Then Hannah prayed: 'My heart rejoiced in the LORD! The LORD has made me strong. Now I have an answer for my enemies; I rejoice because you rescued me.'" I can only imagine her joy and laughter.

Laughter can be a response to surprising and joyous moments in life. I am confident God has laughed at me!

Do you like laughter? Write down something funny that happened recently.

Do you think God laughs? Write down something He did recently to make you laugh.

Do you have a favorite comedian or show you like to watch to laugh? Watch it soon.

If you could color laughter, what color would it be? Draw a smile in that color!

You are gifted.

James 1:17

22

GOD OF MY INTIMACY

I prefer to avoid emotional intimacy, so even thinking of a God of intimacy seems incorrect. That is not how I picture God at all. But I am not talking about the God of sex. I am talking about the God of intimacy. What is this? I am 51 years old, and my eyes have been opened to true intimacy.

What is intimacy? A closeness and vulnerability. I have a closeness with God and with my husband. We always did things together: races, dinner dates, overnights, vacations, etc. We even enjoyed each other's company a lot. It wasn't until we decided to join a program together that helps couples recover from sex/porn addiction that is when I learned what intimacy was. I started understanding true emotional intimacy. We practiced vulnerability by sharing deep emotions from my heart. This was scary to me.

I didn't want the homework that this program offered. It could reveal the real me; what if my husband didn't like the real me? I prefer to wear the mask, for I have done it so well. So had my husband. I tried it, and it has changed me and him. I have learned a lot about intimacy and vulnerability in our 24 months of recovery. I have learned that to get rid of shame, we must talk about it. Expose it to the light. I must share and give it a voice. I must share who I am and my real feelings about it. To be real. No matter the response. The most scary part was being authentic, open, and vulnerable with God. I would say things like, "Well, You already know." And never say my words out loud. Why pray– He already knows.

But having my husband gone left me with no choice but to cry out and be honest with God. I pictured God and me wrestling like He did with Jacob. I also pictured Him rocking with me and cuddling. I started to share my ideas with Him and question what He was doing. I told him I disagreed with how He was handling things. He would say the same to me. We would laugh together. A deeper friendship was developing between me and my Father. True intimacy.

As a child, I was scared God would abandon me. Today, I see I am wrong. He truly is the Faithful One. Now, I can talk, cry, argue, and laugh. He isn't going anywhere, so I can just be me! He has watched me in my cocoon and watched me come out– only to go back in. He's got my back. I am more in love with Him than I was a year ago.

GOD OF MY INTIMACY

But He has always loved me the same. I am finally starting to understand that.

Knowing my needs and desires has been an enormous learning experience for me. I never knew I had needs and desires. Nor did I know I should voice them. I assumed that meant I was being too dependent. I had pushed down who I really was. I ensured my kids' and husband's needs were met as best I could. But not mine. That would have been selfish. Going through this last destruction day, my coach asked me what I needed. Was she serious? She walked me through the fact that it's okay to have needs. She would ask me, "How do you feel about that?" Are you asking me for a feeling? "Fine." I'd say.

As part of our homework, we both had to share F.A.N.O.S:

F - Feelings: Share 1-3 feelings you have.

A - Affirm the other in something.

N - Needs: Share a need you have.

O - Own up to something you did or didn't do.

S - Share a success or struggle.

This was *extremely* hard for me. My husband and I aim to do this daily, and I am much improving (thanks to that feeling wheel). This helps build intimacy with my partner.

Now, because of this, my talks with God are changing.

I have these talks with God and find myself saying back to Him ''That's a great idea!'' I can see Him nodding and smiling. God continues to move mightily in my life; sometimes, He is down at my level, and other times, He shows up so big that I want to fall on my face. Recently, I heard a teaching by Lisa Harper on Luke 11. She says we don't need to ask, beg, or bang on the door for God to hear his child. Because I am His, I can whisper, "Daddy, I need...." He comes closer. He's already near. There is no door between Him and me. I am here, He won't leave. He is by my side.

How do you picture God? What is your relationship like with Him? Let's look at the Bible for who had a deep connection with God:

Moses– He went face to face with God. So bold to ask to see God! That is a bold request! The thought of seeing God makes me tremble. Moses was honest and vulnerable with God.

David– He shared many feelings with God. He was genuine with God, and even genuine with us as he wrote many psalms about his feelings. David was a man after God's own heart.

Elijah– He had amazing encounters with God. He had a bold faith.

Mary– She deeply connected with God just by being Jesus' mom. She was so vulnerable. Her prayer in Luke reveals her heart was willing to obey God right from the beginning.

John– He had such a special connection with Jesus. There was such a closeness. He was the only disciple at Jesus' feet during the crucifixion. Such love he had for Jesus, his friend.

Do you desire intimacy with God?

Start by sharing one feeling a day with God. Share a situation with God and how it makes you feel.

He truly is listening and wants to hear. You are *not* a bother to him; you are His child.

Can anything ever separate us from Christ's love? Does it mean he no longer loves us if we have trouble or calamity, or are persecuted, hungry or destitute, or in danger, or threatened with death? As the Scriptures say, 'For your sake, we are killed every day; we are being slaughtered like sheep.' No, despite all these things, overwhelming victory is ours through Christ, who loved us. And I am convinced that nothing can ever separate us from God's love. Neither death nor life, neither angels nor demons, neither our fears for today nor our worries about tomorrow- not even the powers of hell can separate us from God's love.

Romans 8:35-39 (NLT)

HEALING STEPS

Try sharing with God; Nothing can scare Him away. Trust me, I already tried.

You are seated with Christ.

Ephesians 2:6

23

GOD IS MY FRIEND

Growing up, I thought God was this big mean guy in the sky who, at any moment, would strike me or take my salvation away at the slightest sin. I didn't view him as a friend. The longer I am on this journey, the closer God has come to me. Meeting me where I was– whether that moment was on the bathroom floor crying alone or in the car driving. Wherever I was, I was learning that He was by my side. I started to talk to Him all day—little prayers. I started to have conversations with Him wherever I was. I would think, "Thank God for this bird flying by, '' or ask God to help me find things at the store. I conversed with God in my car as if He was next to me. I'd stand on the deck and say, "What are you doing today, God?" These conversations helped me see God has a friend.

I felt Him compassionately listening as I cried again in the bathroom. He wasn't in the corner looking down, He

HEALING STEPS

was kneeling next to me. I pictured Him rubbing my back. He was drawing near, not distant. He was touching me. His presence was my oxygen. His comfort made me feel safe. My walls were down with Him, and I was learning to be vulnerable with God. Occasionally, I would say ''I am not going to tell you how I feel because you already know," and I would cry or laugh. It seems so silly, but it's so precious. When I woke up, I'd say, "What will today bring?" I almost hear Him say, "Wait and see," or "I got this, Kendra." I was safe. I wasn't walking around alone anymore. He, indeed, was by my side.

The day I called to make an appointment to file for divorce, He was holding my hand while on the phone. He went with me to the lawyer. In the car, I reminded God I did not want to do this. He provided comfort and strength for me that day! You see, my God had gone before me. My lawyer was a godly man and prayed a huge prayer over my situation that morning, surrendering to God's will and begging God to bring my husband back, if it was His will! My lawyer said, "God, we ask for a miracle. It has to be something only you can do, no one else."

My lawyer was safe, understanding, and empathic. I praised God. Right after that meeting, I met a friend for coffee, and she had flowers for me. I felt so taken care of by God! He truly is my friend. He even understands. He understands I need safe friends! Twenty years ago, when I started to share with people my first D-day situation, I learned quickly there aren't many safe people around. I heard the gossip and the horrible and unhelpful advice that sent me home crying. The more D-days I had, the less I told people. I tried to hold it together alone.

Since this last D-day had happened, I had filed for divorce right before Christmas. I decided to wait till January to tell the kids, but I knew I had to tell them immediately because of my husband's actions right after Christmas. With God leading, I organized an emergency family meeting. It was my *worst day ever*. Oh, the tears. I was brave. God held my hand and gave me words to speak. Now, I was asking God to show up for my kids. Their world was shattered, and we were left with nothing but prayer! God was with me, as I told my husband the next day.

This is where the journey truly started. I call this time in my life "My Red Sea journey." This "Red Sea" journey would get darker and scarier. I had no idea the storms that were still brewing. Some days, it felt like the waves were overtaking me; I was drowning. God had this. I knew that much.

We have five kids. I watched them all grieve so differently. My heart broke. Knowing God could meet them *if* they allowed it. I stayed on my knees. I had to allow my kids to grieve and hurt in their own way; it was hard for me. I wanted to scoop everyone up and hold them. I didn't want any of the kids to leave. But allowing these precious children to choose how and what they needed for healing was hard. My heart hurts, and it's hard for a mom to

HEALING STEPS

watch. God was now their healer, parent, and friend. I had to trust God to meet them and comfort them. I continued to pray that we would one day be a family again, whole and healthy. Whatever that looked like.

I had to keep believing that God was working on everyone's heart. I had to be okay with those who couldn't support my family and me. It's not worth getting bitter about, but understanding that some family and friends just can't handle this mess. I get it; I wanted to run from all this, too. But I saw God working and protecting me from unsafe people. The friends who have stayed by my side are the most precious to me, watching me cry at restaurants and reminding me that they love me. They have seen a true change in me from 20 years ago. I think they have been shocked by my "Red Sea ''journey, all the ups and downs of the waves of my sea. They support me because they love me and stay curious about what God is doing or will do. They fight for me and my family on their knees. God has given me safe friends. God cares about friends and family.

Here's what safe friends are to be like:

- Friends encourage us to do our best; friends forgive and help each other in difficult times.

- Friends do not gossip or listen to gossip, allowing it to hurt the friendship. Friends stick around even when things get complicated. They are reliable.

- Friends give pleasant, sincere advice; friends

GOD IS MY FRIEND

honor each other above themselves.

- Friends love each other the same way Christ loves us; friends challenge each other to meet our highest good.

- Friends are not bad-tempered; friends never withhold kindness and mercy.

I have learned to make God my friend. I have learned how to be a (safe) friend to others. I have learned what a true friend is and looks like. I have learned empathy. I have learned what support means.

Let's look at friends in the Bible:

- David and Johnathon: True friendship. Deep friendship, such that when they parted, they experienced true sorrow. What a blessing.

- Ruth and Naomi became friends through a tragedy. I love how God uses trauma to pull us together.

- Elisha and Elijah: They were friends through mentoring and common ground of being a prophet.

- Jesus: He had his 12 disciples. Such a closeness and deep love, a group to be vulnerable with. He knew they had his back. Yet not all of Jesus' family members supported him (John 7:5, Matthew 13:57). How hurtful that must have been, yet that didn't stop him. God always has other plans.

HEALING STEPS

If you ever wonder how to be a compassionate friend, start with listening. Sit and listen with no advice or no questions. Send a gift card or bring a meal over– don't just ask; *do* it without being asked. Or simply just said a card. Heartfelt words go a long way! Be there to accompany them through what they need, whether driving them somewhere or watching their kids.

Make a list of what you need right now, and how you can ask for help. Ponder any friendships you can reach out to for help.

You are God's friend.

John 15:4

24

GOD OF MY WHYS

I was told at a young age not to question God; it was unbelief if I did. But this destruction left me questioning God. I believe God is sovereign, yet I wondered how He could allow this. Why is there free will to sin?

Looking back at Scripture, Genesis 3 records the fall. When all the pain, sin, and suffering enter in, this is why we experience such loss, sickness, and sin. The New Testament is full of verses on suffering. Why did I think I was immune? No one is. Someone once said, "If you haven't had a trial yet, just wait."

As I got older and grew in my faith through smaller trials in my life, I learned God is good enough to allow things to draw me closer to Him. But this trial, in particular, was too much! I was fed up! I have been through five D-days. I have been through too many trickle discoveries (little truths here and there). But it wasn't until after the 3rd D-day that I felt so stuck. Was leaving the marriage wrong?

I hit a horrible low point, so low that no one knew because I don't share emotions; I'm fine. That's when I wrote God a letter, telling Him goodbye, which I shared previously. I was hopeless. It was the scariest time of my life. I trusted no one, not even God. As I returned to my Shepherd, He became even more of a trusted friend. He met, pursued, and kept dumping grace and kindness on me. He was so patient with me. I learned I do need God in my life. I am stronger than I realize. God is my El Roi. I am forever grateful for that time of my life.

I moved from being confused to being changed once again. Until six years later. When the 4th D-day happened, I think my phone must have been listening to the destruction and chaos happening at home because, in my social feed, I was receiving information about betrayal trauma. I signed up that day to take a course to understand what I was going through and what my husband was doing! That course saved and changed my life. I could plant my feet and stand, for I had an understanding of what I was going through now.

What I learned most was that I needed safety, boundaries, and bottom lines. I learned I am strong enough to implement these things. To take care of myself! With God's help, I became empowered. Later that same year when my 5th D-day happened. I had become now well aware

GOD OF MY WHYS

of addiction, how it worked, and why this was happening. I was no longer in betrayal blindness. God continued to transform me into a stronger, more confident person.

My husband knew what would happen if he acted out again, although I am not sure he believed me. I filed for divorce and asked him to leave and get help. It was just me, God, and my "Red Sea" journey, while we were apart. God asked me to surrender, especially my kids. That was the hardest; I didn't want to lose them too! I still threw a fit that all of this was happening. I was angry it happened again. I understood that my God could handle my fit and this situation! He saw me and still loved me. I knew that He was still the judge and jury in this situation. I made my case. He was in charge of my life. I stayed curious and continued to plead my case before Him.

Remember when I talked about God crawling into the cocoon with me? Have you ever studied the changes of a caterpillar? Do you know how dead and decomposed they become *before* the caterpillar moves to the next stage? The caterpillar doesn't just jump into the butterfly stage. It's slowly transformed over time. It decomposes to almost nothing. It's a fantastic process! I knew God wasn't going to allow me to change instantly. Sanctification is a slow, slow process. I knew I was in the slow process of metamorphosis. I wanted to rush into a beautiful butterfly, but God said no. He told me to wait instead. I am an impatient person.

God was slowly killing the old me to bring about change

in my heart. Same with my husband. God knows the right timing to bring about the next stage. There are no rules with Christianity's metamorphosis. We all become butterflies at different times. I had to accept this process and enjoy this cocoon. Only God, my surgeon, does the real heart change.

My aunt always reminds me to quit asking *why*, and ask *who*? Who am I focused on? Changing my perspective from asking God *why* to *who* has helped me stay focused.

I want to look back at many unfair situations in the Bible. Granted, I didn't care about the Bible stories during my D-days. But when you can step back and see the "who" in their lives, it does help to give you hope. Make a list of what was unfair in each person's life:

- Jonah:

- Daniel:

- Joseph:

- Eve:

- Jesus:

When I studied these characters deeply, their lives were hard and not fair, either. What would have happened had they short-changed their process of sanctification? Look at Jonah or Eve, who seemed to have their focus on the *why*. Meanwhile, Daniel, Job, and Joseph focused on the *who*. It's all a matter of our response. I will tell you that Jonah and Eve did get around to the who, but like me, they took

GOD OF MY WHYS

the long route to get there!

I enjoy looking back and seeing how God transformed their lives. I can see what God was doing all along. My situation felt different. I wanted to be able to look back and see God working, not blindly walk this process of betrayal. Moses was angry with God, yet look at what God did through him. What Bible character resonates with you? Are you angry at God? Tell Him.

What is the verse that comforts you the most when you're suffering? What is your perspective today? How would your perspective change *if* you focused on the *who*? Who is your God? My God changes people and situations. He draws near to us in our cocoon. Get comfortable in that cocoon. He's changing you and is capable of handling your situation. You are becoming a butterfly in His time.

You are God's heir.

Romans 8:16-17

25

GOD OF MY TRIGGERS

Triggers are like a bomb that goes off in your brain. Twenty years ago, when I was dealing with this, I was not aware of triggers and PTSD. I was experiencing panic attacks and breakdowns. I asked my husband if this was normal. I begged to go to a mental hospital. What was going on? Today, we know these are normal responses. We know it's a trauma response. My therapist says a D-day is like being in a horrific car accident. Having multiple D-days is like having that same horrific event happen over and over again.

I now understand triggers, and my response to them was my brain protecting me. Pathways in the brain were built during these traumatic events. Trauma, we know, is now stored in the brain and body. When we have any reminders of our D-day, we are thrown back into the past, and our body thinks it's D-day all over again. It's terrifying, and I hate it. I feel powerless. There is no warning! Some days, I have to remind myself what year it is and tell myself that it's not 2021 (when my last D-days were)!

Due to reminders and triggers, I have linked certain things and dates in my head to D-day. I live in fear of specific dates. It can make me become fearful and paralyzed. Pictures/memories can also trigger me. "Oh, he was faithful then," or "He was not faithful here." I wonder if his wedding band was on then? Let's face it. We think we are going crazy when, in fact, we are normal. Our body is seeking safety. I am normal. You are normal.

Let's look at the Bible. Here are a few people I think were probably somewhat traumatized during their life.

The Israelites–They loved God, and then they were done with God. They cried, praised, and then begged to go back to slavery. They needed safety. They faced immense trials and were fearful. This describes me. I had a new everyday life now that I didn't want, and I missed my old normal life that wasn't real. The going back and forth drove me crazy. This left me feeling confused.

David– He spent a lot of his life in hiding. He feared his son and King Saul. Yet he continued to praise and mourn. He went through all the emotions. Like me, he had his back-and-forth cycle that was on repeat.

King Saul– The Bible talks about his moments of

insanity during his life. Saul had so many fears and insecurities.

Job– I can't imagine the trauma he went through. We know God showed up and encouraged him. We know his ending. If you could ask God to show up for you, what would you ask for?

Peter– I wonder what he thought whenever he heard a rooster crow after betraying Jesus. Was he constantly reminded of his sin? What a traumatic event. Such reminders bring us to our knees. Do you think he remembered and felt shame or grace?

A host of Bible characters have been traumatized, from murders to rape. Joseph, Isaac, Tamer, Rahab, Hagar, and Hosea are some who have experienced great trials. Which character do you relate to? Try to understand your triggers. What do you need to help with them?

Someone suggested I make a trigger bag to keep near me. Mine is in the car. I filled it with something for each of my senses to help calm me:

- Sight: My bag
- Smell: Lemon oil
- Touch: Play-Doh
- Taste: Gum
- Hear: Nature

HEALING STEPS

Box breathing has also helped me. You can find how to do that on YouTube.

As for triggers around specific dates, make unique or new plans. Tell a safe person you need extra prayer. How do you feel? What do you need? Go to a new spot or town, grab a friend, or get a massage. Make new memories. Be in tune with your body and what you need.

There is so much more help out there nowadays than there was 20 years ago. I am experimenting with EMDR right now to help me understand and build new pathways in my brain. It seems to help lessen my triggers and help me reframe my thoughts. A betrayal trauma therapist or coach will be a great help to you as you navigate all this! Don't forget to C.A.L.M.

Practice talking to yourself and reassure yourself that you will be okay. I leave myself Post-it notes occasionally, to remind myself I am okay. Suppose you come to my house; you'll find one in my pantry that reminds me I'm a survivor!

Focus on one thing today, something you see right now. Be mindful or meditate on that. What verse comes to mind right now that you can get into your soul? Write it out.

Find time to understand your brain and triggers. Take time to learn about the amygdala. It's a fascinating part of the brain. Its only job is to protect you. It can go into battle mode quickly. It helps you know you're normal when you

GOD OF MY TRIGGERS

have your freak-out moments. It's what your brain was made to do: protect you.

Recently, my husband was away on business; I had an emergency back at home, and he didn't pick up the phone. I am aware that while you're reading this right now, your anxiety went up. Well, my anxiety skyrocketed after 15 phone calls in 15 minutes. When he finally answered, I freaked out. It's hard to even try to respond calmly. My body reacted before my brain. He apologized for breaking a boundary (his phone was turned down while he was out with a colleague). I didn't care what he was doing. He wasn't answering his phone.

That event caused me to be hypervigilant for about three weeks. I had a panic attack twice during that time. My therapist said I went back to 2021 and got stuck. My husband couldn't make any move without a lot of questioning from me. I have since worked through my fears and regained my confidence that if anything were to happen again, I would have a plan B ready to go. I found courage again to move forward into the unknown future. Fear can be so paralyzing. But this trigger set me back and wreaked havoc on my body, brain, and our recovery. It ended up being a teaching moment for both of us. I still can't wait for the day that I can go to a hotel or the doctor's office without being triggered.

God understands your body and brain; He created it. He understands your trauma and what you need. Seek Him;

ask Him to give you understanding. Ask Him to help you with these dates and trauma. God created our bodies and our bodies' response. It's a protection for us! He is with you through the good, bad, and ugly. What do you need when you're being triggered? Make a battle plan of three things you can do in those moments. Aim to achieve one. How can you soak up God's comfort and peace during these times? Draw a picture of that peace.

You are chosen.

John 15:16

26

GOD IS MY LIVING WATER

I only truly understood what living water was once I started studying Hagar. You see, in 2020, we bought our dream house. We were supposed to be downsizing but ended up upsizing. I was excited that my husband finally agreed to move. This would be a fresh start for us. I didn't know that a storm was brewing, and that God was going to use our new house to start the true healing we needed.

I initially wanted a smaller place or a condo. As we looked around, my husband kept finding bigger and bigger houses. I didn't want it to be more significant. But I didn't speak up much because I just wanted to move. So I let him pick. And pick he did. He picked a big house that I didn't want. I was scared of it. So much to upkeep! I knew we didn't have the time for this. But, the owners accepted our offer. I still wasn't sure, so I begged God for a sign.

HEALING STEPS

As I sat in our hot tub outside one morning, I asked God to allow me to see two shooting stars as a sign we were to move. Each morning, I would go out early and look. One morning, I saw two stars shoot across the sky. I ran into the bedroom and said, "I'll move." God showed me.

We moved and then realized how big of a job this house, yard, and pool was. We named our backyard Eucharisteo Gardens. Eucharisteo means joy, grace, and gratitude. Our kids bought us a flag for our flagpole that says Eucharisteo, along with a picture of 2 shooting stars in the corner to attribute how God led us here!

In the summer of 2021 after D-day #4, I struggled to be in this new house. How dare this happen. I was so angry, and it's too much work to keep up with this place anyway; why did we buy it? Why didn't God stop it? But, one day, as I lay on a float in our pool, God pressed on my heart, saying, "You will heal here." I surrendered. I believed and trusted Him. I'm not even sure what those things meant or looked like.

The following summer (in 2022), My husband returned home from a sober living home for sex and porn addicts, when our divorce had been stalled till fall. Once again, God pressed upon my heart: "Your husband will heal here also." This was shocking. So, maybe *this* is why we have this house: to heal. I then told God, that He would have to provide a way to stay living here then! Because the time and money this house required was getting to be too much. Living here was now going to be God's problem.

GOD IS MY LIVING WATER

It wasn't until 2023, going through a study about Hagar, that I learned how God met her by a spring of water. A spring in the desert! Shadia Hrichi wrote in her book *Hagar* that the Hebrew word "spring" is *AYIN*, which can be translated as "eye." She then took me to Jeremiah 9:1 and Lamentations 3:48. How their eyes overflow with tears. My eyes have overflowed with tears, too. Hagar's eyes have overflowed with tears, and guess what? God saw her; God met her at this spring. Shadia continued that Hagar came to the spring scared and left changed by a holy encounter with God himself. She left that spring as a *bold* woman. Shadia then compares it to the women at the well.

The *well*? Another source of water? Yes, Jesus himself encounters her. She felt the same as Hagar: alone, abandoned, and rejected. It's at the well that Jesus tells her He is Living Water. She also leaves changed from her encounter. She was now boldly sharing with others what Jesus had done!

Now, let's circle back to my own house; as I am in deep Bible study over this "living water" concept, I am crying over Hagar and the Samaritan woman. I am in awe of how much God loves and sees women. He makes himself known to both of them. God then pressed upon my heart, "I gave you water too, Kendra." He gave me my Red Sea journey in my backyard. He gave me a huge pool. God, my Living Water, and my pool. God met me and my husband by this water. He wants us to stay here until He tells us. My heart and eyes overflow.

You can read about Hagar's encounter with God in

HEALING STEPS

Genesis 16. Write down any new thoughts or findings. And read about the women at the well in John 4. Does anything new stand out to you?

Don't forget: Jesus is your Living Water! Let Him change you. Seriously, think about this the next time you are near water.

Write out Revelation 7:17.

_____

_____

_____

_____

_____

_____

What feelings come up for you?

_____

_____

_____

_____

You are holy.

Colossians 1:22

27

GOD OF MY GRATITUDE

How does one even appreciate an almighty, powerful, sovereign God? I know God loves our prayers, but what about our praises and thankfulness? Gratitude has changed my life. It has helped my perspectives change. I went from being pessimistic to being optimistic. My demeanor has changed, and people have noticed.

How did I find gratitude? I started by finding one thing a day I can be thankful for. *One.* Some days were hard; I felt I had nothing to be grateful for. Do you know how hopeless that is? I went from being thankful for a dishwasher (which I am) to being grateful for my health, job, and family.

I learned to appreciate how God made me inside and out. I learned to be thankful for my legs and arms, or brain.

I learned to be thankful for my core values, my gift of encouragement, and leadership qualities.

What about your outer qualities can you be thankful for? Now your inner qualities?

Let's turn this to God. Can you name one thing to be thankful for right now? Remind yourself of one thing about who God is. And think, who in the Bible gave thanks to God in tricky situations? I'll list a few:

- David: The Psalms are full of praises to God.

- Job: Job 1:21 reveals Job still praised God amid suffering.

- Daniel: Praised God in Daniel 2 through his prayer.

- Mary: Even in her fear of the unknown, she praised God in Luke 1.

- Paul: He encourages us in Colossians 3 to give thanks for all things.

- Jesus: He gave thanks to God the night he was arrested. Can you imagine?

- Hannah: In 1 Samuel, she offers thanksgiving for her son.

Read Luke 17:11-19. How many lepers were there? How many thanked Jesus?

This kills me. Only one leper thanks Jesus? There's no

GOD OF MY GRATITUDE

gratitude over a cured disease?

Let's move into the importance of praise. I think part of giving glory to God is being thankful and praising Him. Gratitude is a form of praise, but what else is praise?

Turn to 2 Chronicles 20. What happens when Jehoshaphat tells his army to shout praise and hallelujah? Read Joshua 6. What did they do as they ended the last march around the city? Shout! What did they shout? I always wonder if it was a shout of praise. It had to be so sweet to God. What did God do?

John Piper says, "We praise what we prize." What do you prize? How can we pursue a life of praise, and make God be your prize?

We praise as we *Press* in: Train yourself for this race. We praise as we *Persevere*: Endure– don't quit. We praise as we *Persist:* Be determined and keep going strong. Lastly, we praise as we *Prevail*: To the finish line.

Think of ways you can praise God today, and then do them. I encourage you to listen to Brandon Lake's song, "We Praise You."

You are joyful.

Nehemiah 8:18

28

GOD OF MY REDEMPTION STORY

Can God redeem your story? Yes. Will He? Yes. Will He do it when or how you think? Maybe, maybe not. One thing is for sure: *you will be changed*. I will guarantee that. You are already a different person than when you first started to read this book. God is in the business of change and redemption. He does things without asking us permission. One day, we are living a normal life. The next, it's a new chapter. It's beautiful, it's scary, and it's painful.

My own story of change progressed slowly over twenty years. Although I unknowingly married a sex-addict, God used the suffering and trials our marriage has endured to provide a rich transformation in my life. Graciously, God allowed me a "breather' between D-days to prepare me for the next round. God was slowly building my character and my faith muscle. He is so patient with me.

I went from suffering alone to vulnerability. My view of God has changed. My view of myself has changed. I know who I am. Today, I see myself as a precious jewel. I am a gift. I choose now to operate out of my core values instead of out of fear.

Can God redeem your marriage? Yes. I believe He is redeeming mine. He has given me a man who is still seeking after God, who is praying about everything, working on recovery, and helping keep me safe. Secretly, I made a list of what I wanted in a new man and brought it before God. I stayed curious. Maybe God won't change your spouse or marriage; maybe He is protecting you and telling you to get out. This takes much prayer and wisdom to navigate. God gives grace and strength for the road to stay or the road to go. This is between you and God.

Before he came home from his five months away, my husband asked me if I would do a three-day intensive with him. He was willing to do a full disclosure, telling me everything that had happened over our entire marriage. Being completely honest with me and agreeing to a polygraph. I agreed hesitantly.

Hearing his full disclosure was one of the worst days of my life. It put me in emotional ICU with a broken heart. I do believe it laid the foundation – an honest foundation – for a new beginning. It validated so much of what I had wondered. My gut had been right all along. I was grateful to have a sincere, truth-telling husband! We started that new journey in the summer of 2022. Since then, I have read an impact letter to him of all the ways his secret life had impacted my life, its twenty pages. It was a hard letter to write, but it was also empowering to read. A few months later, he gave me a beautiful restitution letter, stating his ownership and responsibility of all the impacts his sin and addiction had on my life. He acknowledged and validated everything I had written in my impact letter. He shared in my grief and shared his remorse. He ended it with what he was going to do as he moved forward and shared hopes and dreams of becoming a man of God. It was beautiful.

Since then, he has now had four polygraphs, and will continue those yearly for my own safety. Recovery, I have heard, is at least five years long. We aren't even halfway. Yes, we are tired, but we aren't quitting. We are both fighters. We are doing the daily homework and weekly homework. We each have a sex addiction therapist, and in January 2022, I agreed to couples emotional-focused therapy (E.F.T.). We are both becoming new (like a butterfly). It's like we each get a new spouse– which is so weird.

We continue to find out new things about each other. We are trying new hobbies together. We are learning to respect each other mutually. We have become better friends and better at emotional intimacy. We also respect each other's need for space. Both of us have, most importantly, continued to let the Potter (God) shape our lives. Little did

I know that when I dared God to restore us, I wouldn't just get a restored husband– he would get a restored wife!

Let's look at a few stories in the Bible where reconciliation did *not* happen.

- Cain and Abel
- David and Saul
- David and Absalom
- Judas and the disciples

These friendships have a common theme of death, which makes this scary to me; they are so tragic. David had to learn to go on without any form of reconciliation. The disciples were left in shock and pain at the betrayal of Judas, whom they loved as a trusted friend.

As we navigate the painful journey of betrayal trauma, some of us have experienced the loss of support from friends and perhaps even family members. Occasionally, God removes people from our lives either permanently or temporarily. I have experienced this. It hurts. It's shocking. But, respecting people is to allow them to leave if they so desire. Sometimes, people have expectations of others. For me, maybe they expected me to perform, do certain things, or take their advice. Maybe they are mad that I am fighting for my marriage. It could be jealousy of my boundaries. I can't fix or control them. I am not called to listen to them. I am called to honor and listen to my Savior. God will pull

GOD OF MY REDEMPTION STORY

people out of your life for His purpose. Looking back at who He pulled out of my life, I now say thank you. He was protecting me.

Do you have someone who has left your side? How does it make you feel? It could have brought up feelings of being a contagious leper again, hurt and abandoned. Why do you think God is allowing this? Will you trust what God is doing?

I am sure David questioned why he lost Jonathan. Jesus understands loss. He lost his friend Lazarus. Paul almost lost his friend Epaphroditus. They were restored after he got well.

God knows what people we need in our lives and what people we don't need. He doesn't ask us. He allows it to happen. You may not understand now, but in time you will.

There are numerous stories about redemptions out there. All are such miracles. And there are numerous stories where people are changed, but marriages are not restored. All are part of His plan. I think it's about giving God glory while you walk whatever path He puts you on. We can praise God on any road. Stay faithful and stay curious.

Let's look now at where restoration did happen in the Bible:

- The prodigal son was restored to his family.

- Joseph was restored to his family.

HEALING STEPS

- Jacob and Esau made amends.

- Jesus seeks out Peter for restoration.

Which one of these stories gives you hope? Does this encourage you to feel hope, even if your situation seems hopeless? Do you believe God can work in hopeless situations?

Look back at the patriarchs. There was much learning, growing, and changing; things didn't turn out in a big bow. But they were all changed for God's glory. Their faith grew.

Draw a picture of two roads. One leading to what you want– write that above your road.

It could be that you want a new car, a different or a new wedding band. Anything you want. Then, draw a road of things you don't want. You could even list your marriage on either road. Draw God or the heavens at the top of the page. And draw a picture of yourself smiling underneath God.

No matter what road you're on, you will be okay. You will learn to thrive because you are a survivor. We can have the courage to step into the unknown. Taking a risky step of faith will help overcome your fears. I bravely took a leap of faith in overcoming my relationship fears about whether to stay or leave. Eventually, I came to the realization that I would be alright no matter which path I chose. I found comfort in knowing that God will always be by my side.

GOD OF MY REDEMPTION STORY

We took a risky step of faith with buying this house. We arrived at Eucharisteo Gardens dead; we just didn't know it. Over the last 4 years we have become fully alive and healed. God truly has turned our graves into gardens! Jesus does bring life to the dead! Look up these verses for hope and encouragement:

Ezekiel 37:1-14, Isaiah 61:4, and Psalm 30:10-12

Do you believe God has you? Sit back and watch Him work. Because whether you believe it or not, God does have you. And He won't let you go. Listen to "Graves into Gardens" by Elevation Worship.

You are a beautiful crown.

Isaiah 62:3-4

HEALING STEPS

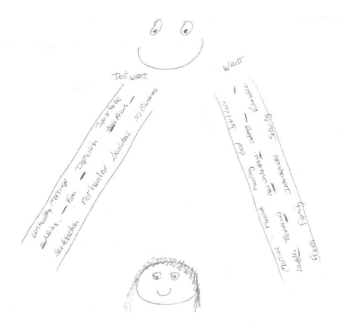

29

GOD OF MY MIRACLES

Yes, God still does miracles. I have fully witnessed it. When I went to file for divorce, my attorney was determined that God still does marriage miracles. I never saw such faith. He explained what a miracle was– something only God can do, in order that God can get glory, not man. I wasn't looking for a miracle; I just wanted out. I was at the end of my rope. My lawyer told me I prayed for two miracles: my husband's heart change, and my own heart, also. I didn't see that happening, but it kept me curious, so I prayed before God. I realize even changing *one* heart is a big miracle. Seriously, taking a dead person and making them alive is such a precious miracle. But two hearts changed? It seemed even more unrealistic than the two shooting stars I asked for in 2020.

God was at work in my heart even before I saw my attorney. Years ago, I received a tremendous miracle in

2010. I had already gone through 2 D-days, and I was still trying to fix my husband by looking for a list of rules. I was steeped in legalism. In therapy, she told me, "You don't understand grace." I was so angry with her. Who are you to say such an evil thing? She suggested I study grace before my next visit. I was clueless. Where do I start? I could tell you the definition of grace. But, truly, I didn't know grace, just truth.

The understanding happened a week later. I will never forget that day as I was studying Romans 2. I was on my bed reading verse 4: "Kindness leads to repentance." I was shocked. *What?* I remember the blinders coming off my eyes. Seriously, I felt the Holy Spirit pull them off. I lay there with a heavy heart, crying and sobbing. Then I got up to tell everyone my newfound discovery! Did you know how much grace God gives you even when you disobey? Did you know He uses kindness, not shame, to draw you to Him? I will never forget it. That day changed me.

My friends, kids, and husband saw me change. I threw legalism out the window that day! I haven't looked back. I try to use kindness whenever possible to show God's glory! Looking back, I see God was working on me to prepare me for a profound work. Where would I be without His grace and my understanding of grace? Where would I be without His forgiveness? Having my eyes opened helped me read the Bible differently, as I was studying Jeremiah, Israel, adultery, and divorce. I remember sobbing as the Holy Spirit showed me that I, too, had committed adultery.

I, too, had been unfaithful to my God.

I was so overcome with emotion that all I could do was sob. I had sinned; I still sin. That day showed me that if I can be unfaithful to God, I can indeed be unfaithful in my marriage. I was overcome with gratitude for God's grace, mercy, and love for me. It's been God's grace that I haven't been unfaithful, and it's God's grace that I will continue to be faithful to Him and my marriage.

2010 wasn't my only miracle. I received many more in 2022. As I look back in my journal of this "Red Sea" journey through destruction starting in December 2021, I started to write down my bold prayers; I prayed for everything! I then highlighted all my answers and miracles. Guess what? I have over thirty-five miracles recorded! I started to cry.

God has shown up in providing ways for my kids and providing for our family vacations. I saw how God provided extra pay in the paycheck when God knew I booked a family trip by faith. Another one was when my husband was down south healing, the small group leaders that took my husband in were from the same town we were living in now! Isn't it just like my God to orchestrate such things? I remember asking God in 2021 to do something outrageous; I needed to see this. I asked God if He could sell the company my husband worked for. Like seriously, I was asking *big*. It ended up selling over a year later, and then they merged/bought another one. I was left awestruck. I love to ask God little things, too, like when I need to see a butterfly or shooting stars. It's such a minor thing to ask for, yet so beautiful.

Here are some other miracles I have experienced:

- When my 5th D-day hit, I asked God for prayer partners in 2021. God gave me over fifty! So many were strangers, but now they're close friends who still check in on us!

- My daughter asked me if we could stay in the house till she graduates. I said let's pray about it. I didn't know if me and my husband would be divorcing before then. But we just celebrated her graduation party here. God was working and answering. He's so kind to us.

- Recently, my husband thought he would end the quarter with no deals. At 5 pm, I quit praying, but guess what? At 8 pm on a Friday, two deals closed. We sat there with our mouths open.

- My daughter has a friend who was very sick. No one knew what was wrong. Now she's healed.

- My son sold his house for *more* than he was asking (even though I was praying against this sale because it meant he would move out of state, which he did).

- God provided a car for my child.

- I had asked God to get the affair partner out of the way! He did. Thank you, God (I still am praying for a miracle of her soul).

GOD OF MY MIRACLES

- My husband chose to get sober on January 26, 2022. Truly a miracle. He got a sponsor and joined the S.A.A. group. He's two years sober. Still working on 12 steps! It's still a miracle!

- A grandchild (a rainbow baby) was born while my husband was away. She is such a redemption baby.

Does God answer all prayers the way we want? Nope. Does He still do miracles? *Yes.* What miracles have you seen? What miracles do you need to ask God for? Ask big and ask bold. Don't relent.

What's your favorite miracle in the Old Testament? I love all that happened when the Israelites wanted to escape Egypt. They seem so outrageous when I read them. How God works gives me goosebumps. I love the parting of the Red Sea.

What's your favorite miracle in the New Testament? Mine is when Jesus turned water into wine. Jesus knows the importance of food and fellowship. He hears his mother's request for more wine, tells her it's not His time, yet does it; for it seems to honor His mother.

I am reminded of Romans 4:17: "The God who gives life to the dead and calls into being things that were not".

I love this. Reread it; what two things does God do? That's the God we serve.

Keep an eye out for God, no matter how big or small.

HEALING STEPS

He is always on the move. Start writing this down! Don't miss it. Stay curious. Listen to "Million Little Miracles" by Elevation Worship.

You are a miracle.

Psalm 139:13-15

30

GOD OF MY FORGIVENESS

This is the last chapter I'm writing. I was praying and asking God, "What shall I say in this chapter?" He didn't hesitate to impress forgiveness on my heart. I winced and shook my head. I have no way of writing about it. Have I done it? Yes, in the past. Have I experienced the freedom forgiveness brings? Yes. I still don't want to touch it. Why? It's tricky. I wish there was a formula.

Over the years, I have been given horrible advice: you must forgive as soon as possible and never bring it up again. I fell for that advice. The effects it had on my body and emotions were not healthy. My heart wasn't ready, for I hadn't processed any of my feelings. What this addiction did to me over most of my marriage was so severe that I realized I would need time.

HEALING STEPS

I needed to give the Holy Spirit time to work on me, but my counsel wanted to rush this process. I tried to forgive, but it didn't stick. I tried not to bring anything up, but that wasn't working, due to PTSD. Why couldn't I forgive and move on? I didn't want bitterness to take root.

Years later, I am learning how forgiveness is a process. I needed to give myself grace and space to let God work on my heart. I told God years ago that I never wanted to experience such pain ever again. I never want to grant forgiveness like that again. Whenever I heard the song "Oceans" by Hillsong on the radio, I would turn it off and shake my head. I will never go that deep, ever again. I see now that God took my stubbornness as a challenge.

The thought of forgiveness makes me feel anxious. Who has time to dig deep and put forth that effort? I will tell you that I have seen the effects of unforgiveness, though. It's ugly. You become critical and mean. I believe unforgiveness will take you down into a deep pit. I didn't want that either.

What I do know is that forgiveness is a choice; it's not a feeling. I know how good it feels to forgive, though. The freedom that comes with it is life changing. I know granting forgiveness hurts for a moment. It feels powerful to keep that hurt, but that's a lie. It's not powerful, it's destructive. The real power is releasing that hurt by forgiving. The Holy Spirit does amazing things between people when we grant forgiveness. During forgiveness, both parties receive a gift.

GOD OF MY FORGIVENESS

So, when I felt pressed to talk about forgiveness, I found a secular course on forgiveness. I knew what the Bible said, but what about the world? Let me quote from the web course, *Self Healers' Circle* on forgiveness.

> Forgiveness is the act of letting go and releasing all of one's feelings/emotions- i.e., pain, anger/resentment, jealousy, fear, etc. after a perceived wrong, unfair or hurtful treatment or otherwise harmful experiences. When we are truly willing and able to do so, there is a direct impact on our heart, body, thoughts, feelings, reactions and how we show up are expressed in the world. While many of us have learned to associate forgiveness with the involvement of another, forgiveness is truly a gift we give to ourselves and for ourselves. It begins with yourself.
>
> We can only truly forgive ourselves and others when we are connected to our own heart and how we feel about our experiences; only then can we acknowledge, let go of, and choose to release its impact.

I do agree we ourselves need to feel to heal. However, connecting to God is the only way to fully release and heal. Forgiveness honors God. But honestly, the things I have had to forgive would be impossible without the Holy Spirit.

After I took this small course on forgiveness, I would

HEALING STEPS

write about it. Yet God, once again, impressed my heart that I should be vulnerable and real.

So, here we go. In the summer of 2021, after what I thought was the last D-day, I took a 12-week betrayal trauma course, and the topic of forgiveness came up. This is the same time Lysa Terheurst came out with her course, *Forgiving What You Can't Forget*. I then purchased the book and study guide. I took her course, ate up the materials, and went into battle. I highly recommend it if/when you have time for soul searching.

Anyway, when I finished the course, I checked into a hotel and spent the night with God, reading and studying. Lysa had these cards at the end of the book to fill out. Listing all the people I needed to forgive. I went through my childhood, high school days, old church issues, and my husband's offenses. When I was done, I had over 60 cards filled out. I then lit a candle in the dark room, prayed, and released each person. It took me a while. But when I was done, I felt such a release and freedom. When my husband came to pick me up, I told him I forgave him. Did I trust him yet? No, but my faith was moving forward.

He then took me to dinner, and we celebrated what God was doing. Isn't this beautiful? I wish I could end there, but it doesn't end there. Well, you know my story got worse. My husband's addiction was getting the better of him, and he let it take over. He had considered leaving me and starting over elsewhere. What did God do? He took me deep into the ocean of troubles without my permission. Because, by the end of 2021, I had filed for divorce. Did I regret forgiving that previous summer?

Never. Because we were both becoming new people with a renewed marriage. I ended up canceling the divorce almost a year after filing. We both are so hopeful and grateful.

Have I forgiven? I'm still in the process. Am I willing? Absolutely. God is teaching me so much right now. My husband continues to work on amends with me, which is what I need to move forward in my healing. I am writing this because God draws me into what His will is. God has also used some of those secular courses to give me understanding. God uses it all. A full forgiveness is coming! I promise. God will see to it! He will get me there!

What about you? Have you ever forgiven anyone? How did it make you feel? Do you have unforgiveness now? How does that make you feel? Are you scared to release the hurt? This is normal; I am, too. Make a promise to yourself to at least pray about forgiveness.

As for forgiving the church, this one is hard because I have higher expectations of church leaders. I recently have worked through forgiving the pastor who gave me bad advice while I was 16 and pregnant. I did this through E.M.D.R. I realized that church leaders are human. They make mistakes. We are all called to love the unlovable. I am unlovable, my husband is, and the church is also. This is why Jesus came, right? But I feel pain for so many hurting wives. I feel outraged and sad. I have heard from many of you women who share their stories of how their church leaders did not support or validate them. They were told to "submit" to their husbands and the church authority. They were placed in grave danger. Their children and husbands were also. Many women have not only been abandoned by their husbands but also by the church. This must grieve God. To go through betrayal and church abandonment is horrific. Many women have stepped away from their faith due to church hurts. My only hope is Ezekiel 34.

I must learn to surrender the hurt and pain. I know my God sees and will vindicate me and many other hurting families in His time. I am called to forgive. This process I am on is taking me there. My therapist suggests that I write an "empty chair" letter. Write what I would say to the church leaders, get it all out, read it to an empty chair, and then release it or burn it. I am in the writing phase now and won't run away. I want to heal fully. God is walking me gently through the process of forgiving. I am scared but ready.

I love this quote by St. Augustine, "Resentment is like drinking poison and waiting for the other person to die." What are your thoughts after reading this? Do you believe it is true? Be courageous enough to ask God to show you what your next step should be. Ask God to protect your heart from bitterness as you work through forgiveness.

GOD OF MY FORGIVENESS

Thank you, God, for granting us forgiveness.

You are forgiven.

Isaiah 1:18

Listen to "Same God" by Hannah Kerr

*May God give you wings
in that cocoon to fly away and flourish!*

EPILOGUE

As for my cream wedding dress? God did a work in my heart in 2010 as I realized I no longer needed to wear that coat of shame. I realized Jesus has me wrapped in His white robe of righteousness. As I was crying and sharing my revelation about that dress with my children, my precious daughter #3 surprised me with a white wedding dress from Goodwill. She wanted me to own a *white* dress. I couldn't quit crying. What a precious gift this was to me! I said my final goodbye to the cream dress and burned it in the summer of 2022. It was very freeing. I anxiously await Jesus' return when I will wear the biggest, prettiest, most beautiful white dress ever! He sees me as *pure*.

AFTERWARD

Kendra continues to help other women with her story. Her goal is to bring encouragement and hope. She loves to coach others through this journey of pain to healing. To let others know how *big* God is. She wants others to know that they are "seen" by a Holy God. She is still healing and believes God can heal anyone.

> *But as for me, I know that my Redeemer lives,*
> *and he will stand up on the earth at last.*
> *And after my body has decayed,*
> *yet in my body I will see God!*
> *I will see him for myself. Yes, I will see him with my own eyes.*
> *I am overwhelmed at the thought!*
>
> **Job 19:25-27(NLT)**

As for her husband, he continues to work on his recovery plan as a top priority. He also continues to pursue healing. He recently completed a Family of Origin intensive. He is two years sober and so grateful for God's rescue, his sponsors, his S.A.A. groups, and tools to help him on his journey of transformation. His desire is to help other men and give them hope; addiction doesn't have to win.

As for their marriage, they are getting to know each other again since they both have changed. They still do

HEALING STEPS

daily and weekly recovery homework together. Once a year, they meet together with a therapist for a "check-up" and do a polygraph.

APPENDIX

Find me on Facebook: KENDRA LEE

YouTube: @CoachKendraLee

TikTok:@kendra.lee12

My Linktree: linktr.ee/coachkendralee

Websites:

www.partnerhope.com

www.affairrecovery.com

www.brave1.com

www.recoveredpeace.com

www.hopeandfreedom.com

www.room2heal.org

www.relationalrecovery.com

www.daringadventures.com

www.bloomforwomen.com

www.sexhelpwithcarolthecoach.com

www.apsats.org

www.living-truth.org

www.btr.org

www.sanon.org

www.cosa-recovery.org

HEALING STEPS

www.isurvivors.org

www.recovering-couples.org

www.celebraterecovery.org

www.saa.org

Books:

Out of the Shadows- Understanding sex addiction by Patrick Carnes

The Betrayal Bind by Michelle Mays

Facing Heartbreak by Stephanie Carnes

Unleashing Your Power by Carol Juergenson Sheets

Your Sexually Addicted Spouse by Barbara Steffens

Fight for Love by Rosie Mckinney

The Body Keeps Score by Bessel Van Der Kolk.

In Sheep's Clothing by George Simon

Intimate Deception by Sherri Keffer

Study of Lamentations by thedailygrace.com

Grief by Tim Keller

Unattended Sorrow by Stephen Levine

Journals by Serena K Phoenix on Amazon:

Healing Horizons mindset journal for trauma recovery

APPENDIX

Healing Hearts Kids mindset journal for trauma recovery

My Trigger journal

Recommended Youtube videos:

Forgiveness by Eva Kor- A holocaust survivor

How betrayal affects the brain by Jake Porter

The brain science of partner betrayal by Sex help with Carol the coach

F.A.N.O.S.

Podcasts:

Helping Couples Heal

RecoverU

Fight for Love

Hope for Wives

FEELINGS

HAPPY-Joy, proud, accepted, powerful, peaceful, optimistic, amused, confident, important, loving, hopeful, playful, open, inspired.

SURPRISE-Excited, amazed, confused, awe, eager, energetic, shocked, startled, shocked, dismissed.

FEAR-Humiliated, rejected, insecure, scared, terrified, worried, overwhelmed, worthless, inadequate, disrespected.

ANGER-Hurt, mad, aggressive, hateful, frustrated, distant, critical, embarrassed, devastated, resentful, jealous, insecure, hostile, irritated, suspicious, skeptical.

DISGUST-Loathing, awful, avoidance, disappointment, judgment.

SAD-Guilty, despair, lonely, abandoned, bored, depressed, ashamed, ignored, powerless, vulnerable, inferior, empty, indifferent.

From the book, *Your Sexually Addicted Spouse*
by Barbara Steffens

Here's a list of betrayal trauma symptoms:

Hyperarousal

Panic attacks

Oversensitivity

Dissociation

Reliving the event

Health problems

Helplessness

Hypervigilance

Intrusive thoughts

Withdrawing

Phobias

Depression

Inability to eat

Chronic Fatigue

Sleeplessness

Anxiety

Avoidance

Flashbacks

Restlessness

Overeating

Immune/endocrine issues

Immobility

Nightmares

Mood swings

Denial

Confusion

Rage

SELF-CARE IDEAS

Meet up with a friend

Bake a treat

Go to the spa

Color or Paint

Read a book

Listen to a podcast

See a movie

Cry

Put on makeup

Try something new

Take a bubble bath, shave your legs

Get a weighted blanket

Light a candle

Yoga

Eat your favorite food

Turn off your phone

Work in the garden

Try a new restaurant

Mow

Buy a new outfit

Get a body scan

Look at the sunrise/sunset

Be still

Rearrange your room

Write a letter to a loved one

Buy flowers

Get some fresh air

Order in your favorite meal

Start a new skincare routine

Go for a walk

Cuddle with a pet

Write in your journal

Turn off the T.V.

Drink coffee or tea

Donate to a cause

Text someone you love

Drink more water

Take some deep breaths

Clean out your inbox

Listen to your favorite music

BIBLIOGRAPHY

Hrichi, Shadia. *HAGAR*. Abilene, TX: Leafwood publishers, 2017

Le Pera, Nicole. https://theholisticpsychologist.com/. www.selfhealerscircle.com.

Mays, Michelle. *The Betrayal Bind: How to Heal When the Person You Love the Most Hurts You the Worst*. Central Recovery Press, 2023.

Perkins, Zachary. "4 people who successfully argued with God." *Relevant*, June 3, 2014. https://relevantmagazine.com/faith/4-people-who-successfully-argued-god/.

Piper, John. *Future Grace, Revised Edition: The Purifying Power of the Promises of God*. Multnomah, n.d.

Seeking Integrity. "Debbie McRae, Processing Anger, 2.16.24," February 19, 2024. https://www.youtube.com/watch?v=ebHmodPw44k.

Terkeurst, Lysa. *Forgiving What You Can't Forget*. Nashville, TN: Thomas Nelson, 2020.

Youversion bible app. Tyndale publishers

ABOUT THE AUTHOR

Kendra is a wife, mother, grandmother, personal fitness trainer, and certified recovery coach. She is an early bird. She starts her day with a 3:30 am coffee and a date with God. When she is not working, she is with her grandkids or catching up with a friend. She looks forward to her weekly date nights with her husband, and she loves seeing movies, traveling, and eating out, especially now that she's an empty nester. Recently, Kendra and her husband celebrated their 35th wedding anniversary. She will tell you it's *only* God's grace.

Printed in the USA
CPSIA information can be obtained
at www.ICGtesting.com
CBHW071716050724
11187CB00037B/978